Rodger D. Eakin
Room 213 Hail Hill.
Box 240
Belmont College
Nashville, Tenn.

THE POETRY OF THE
OLD TESTAMENT

By the same Author:

PROPHECY AND THE PROPHETS
IN ANCIENT ISRAEL

THE POETRY OF THE OLD TESTAMENT

By

THEODORE H. ROBINSON

Litt.D. (*Cantab.*); *D.D.* (*Lond.*); *Hon. D.D.* (*Aberdeen*);
Hon. D.Th. (*Halle*);
Emeritus Professor of Semitic Languages, University College, Cardiff

GERALD DUCKWORTH & CO. LTD.
3 HENRIETTA STREET, LONDON, W.C.2

First published in 1947
Reprinted 1952, 1960

MADE AND PRINTED IN GREAT BRITAIN BY
BURLEIGH LIMITED AT THE BURLEIGH PRESS
BRISTOL

CONTENTS

To
W. O. E. OESTERLEY
TO WHOSE SCHOLARSHIP, COLLABORATION, AND
FRIENDSHIP THE AUTHOR OWES SO MUCH,
THIS LITTLE BOOK IS AFFECTIONATELY DEDICATED

PREFACE

THE following pages contain the substance of a course of lectures delivered in alternate years at Cardiff over a quarter of a century. They are not a transcript of the lectures given in any one year. For one thing, no written copy exists. For another, a good deal had to be given to University students which is quite unnecessary for the general public, especially in tracing the scientific study of Hebrew poetic form.

The book is, then, a summary of results reached in forty years' study of the poetry found in the Old Testament. Yet it is very far from being what I would have wished it to be, and if I had any hope of improving it, I would have postponed publication still further. There is one section in particular where I feel the inadequacy of my work, and that, to many readers, the most important of all. The truth is that the study of the Psalter had been thrown into the melting-pot by the researches and theories of Gunkel and others, and it may be many years before the adherents of the fresh view-point settle down to a consistent and agreed position. In the circumstances I have felt that the best course was merely to summarize roughly Gunkel's classification, with some reference to the work done by a few others. Any reader who wishes to go further into the matter may consult the books recommended in the Bibliography at the end of this volume.

It remains to perform the very pleasant duty of thanking

all on whose help I have been able to rely in the production of this little book. To mention all the countless numbers who have contributed in one way or another would be impossible, and my apologies are hereby offered to any reader who resents omission from the list. But there are one or two who stand out.

First, George Buchanan Gray, that great scholar who passed from us nearly twenty-five years ago. Not only by his writings (and his *Forms of Hebrew Poetry* is still the great classic on the subject), but by direct discussion, he gave me such insight as I have into the basic principles which underlie what we call Hebrew Metrics. Next, two of my former colleagues in Cardiff. Chapter I of this book is based on notes of a lecture given by Mr. E. C. Llewellyn, Professor of English in University College, Cardiff, and he has been good enough to read the typescript and satisfy himself that his views have not been seriously misrepresented. To him also I owe a number of suggestions, and the section of the Bibliography which deals with Chapter I. My debt to Professor A. R. Johnson is even greater. Him I have to thank, not only for years of happy co-operation in the teaching of Hebrew, but for innumerable suggestions, both general and particular, for the book itself. I wish it had been possible to incorporate more fully the results of his own research, but all who know him look forward to the time when he will lay them before the wider public. With the exception just mentioned, the Bibliography is almost entirely his work, and from it readers may get a faint conception of all I owe him. Finally he has read the proofs with that meticulous care and passion for accuracy which characterises all his work. One other must be mentioned ; my wife has not only been beside me during the years when this book was actually being written, but has read with me the proofs, as she has done in the case of nearly every work I have published.

And so this work goes out, with the hope and the prayer that it may help some others to grasp a little from that marvellous treasury of divine revelation which is enshrined for us in the poetic sections of the Word of God.

THEODORE H. ROBINSON.

Ealing, *October, 1946.*

A*

I

PROSE AND POETRY

MOST of us know the difference between poetry and prose.
When we hear or see a passage we have no difficulty in
deciding to which class of literature or of speech it
belongs. Conventionally and very conveniently, poetry
is written in definite lines, each of which is, as it were, a
complete whole, and in one way or another stands apart
from what precedes and from what follows. It is not
always the sense of the line which is thus isolated ; often
it runs on continuously through a number of lines, and
may not end at the conclusion of a line or even of a group
of lines. So Milton began *Paradise Lost :*

> Of man's first disobedience, and the fruit
> Of that forbidden tree whose mortal taste
> Brought death into the world, and all our woe,
> With loss of Eden, till one greater Man
> Restore us and regain the blissful seat,
> Sing, Heavenly Muse, . . .

We can read this in two quite different ways, either line
by line or as a single sentence, but if we make our greater
pauses at " fruit," " taste," or " man," we shall make
nonsense of the sentence. Again, when Tennyson wrote :

> Let knowledge grow from more to more,
> But more of reverence in us dwell,
> That mind and soul according well,
> May make one music as before

> But vaster. We are fools and slight . . .

he certainly did not intend us to connect " But vaster " closely with the next words.

Poetic form, however, is dependent on something more than a line-by-line arrangement. If these two passages had been written continuously, without being divided into lines, we should still have realised that they were not ordinary prose, as soon as we read them aloud, or permitted ourselves to think of their sound. They make an impression on us which is entirely different from that which is produced by normal speech. As a rule we do not stop to analyse that impression ; we are content to accept it, but if we are to understand the real difference between prose and poetry, we must go further and see why we are affected differently by the two forms.

We can see at once that no small part is played by the diction, the choice and arrangement of words. It is possible to present the outward form without giving the inner spirit which pervades all true poetry. Suppose, for example, some one were to say to us :

> " It's getting rather late,
> I hear them shouting for me,
> I'm going to start at half-past eight,
> I hope it won't be stormy."

The doggerel verse would either annoy or amuse us according to our temperament or mood, but none of us would think of it as poetry. But put the same thought into other words, as the real poet does, and we get :

> " Sunset and evening star,
> And one clear call for me,
> And may there be no moaning at the bar
> When I put out to sea."

At once we are lifted out of the realm of common things, and are transported into something which is indescribable.

The words are all familiar and natural, yet the genius of the writer has so handled them that they convey to us a meaning which transcends all power of verbal expression.

At the same time we must realise that great prose may have much the same kind of effect, and that, too, without having recourse to obscure or " pretty " words. Few of us can ever forget, even if we cannot quote, Lincoln's Gettysburg speech or his second inaugural address. In the first chapter of Froude's *History of England* there is a passage—two paragraphs only—beginning " For, indeed, a change was coming upon the world, the meaning and direction of which is still hidden from us, a change from era to era . . ." The dignity and beauty of this short section give us a background, partly emotional and partly intellectual, against which we see the whole of the story unfolding as we read the twelve volumes of the work. Again, on reading it, we pass through an experience which we cannot even describe, still less explain, in ordinary language.

We come back, then, to the form as being that which is distinctive of poetry as contrasted with prose. And at once we are faced with a variety of forms in different languages. The earliest Greek poetry we know depended on the alternation of long and short syllables, and their various arrangements. We still have short pieces of Latin poetry surviving from an age earlier than that at which it was influenced by Greek, and the form appears to depend on the accent of the words. The well-known classical poets, of course, abandoned the native method and adopted that of Greece, a process possible in Latin though it has seldom been a success when attempted in the languages of modern Europe, where, indeed, it is hardly possible to make the distinction between long and short syllables a basis for poetic form at all.

Another common feature in poetic form is the use of similar sounds, either at the beginning or at the end of the lines. Anglo-Saxon poetry, for example, depended for its form on " alliteration " ; a line was divided into two parts, and two words in the first part, together with one in the second, began with the same consonantal or any vowel sound. French poetry, and much in other languages, such as English, German, Italian and Spanish, is marked by similar sounds at the ends of successive or alternating lines. This is what we call " rhyme," and it may be employed in a variety of ways. Sometimes two consecutive lines will rhyme, sometimes alternate lines, and sometimes the arrangement is still more complicated. We may have a scheme which we can indicate as a.a., b.b., etc. Another may be a.b., a.b., or we may have such a scheme as that used by Dante in *La Divina Comèdia* —a.b.a., b.c.b., c.d.c. . . ., which serves to link successive groups of three lines each. In many lyric poems we get still more complicated arrangements, too numerous to mention.

In several modern languages, the poetic form takes no notice either of alliteration or of rhyme. Instead it concentrates on the relation of accented to unaccented syllables. Naturally, the effectiveness of such an arrangement depends in large measure on the strength of the accent, and it is best suited to languages like English or German, where the stress placed on the dominant syllable is fairly strong. As a rule the particular metres which are formed on this basis resemble those of the ancient Greek and Latin prosodies, the stressed syllable taking the place of the " long," and the unstressed that of the " short." The names applied to the classical feet are used, and we can speak of the iambus or of the dactyl, though we should remember that it is really a very different thing in each case from that for which the term was originally invented. People who speak English may read

"But thee I now would serve more strictly, if I may." much as they would read an iambic line from a Greek dramatist, forgetting that the accents in the latter often fall on short syllables, and have no bearing on the actual metre.

Languages in which the accent is too weak to be impressive usually concentrate either on rhyme (as in French) or on the comparative length of the syllables (as in Arabic). But in all these cases the number of syllables is significant, and there are forms of poetry in which it is the counting of these syllables alone which is considered. Such a case is to be found in Syriac, where, however, rhyme often plays a part, or in some of the Sanskritic languages.

What is there in common between all these different types of poetic scheme? Surely it is the principle of *regularity*? This need not be absolute, indeed it seldom is. Only an expert can really appreciate the metres of the choric odes used in Greek drama, and there the highly complicated scheme of the strophe is repeated only once, in the antistrophe. But it should not be forgotten that the singing of these lyrics was accompanied by a dance, and that the movement and the sound went closely together, thus strengthening the effect which either might produce alone. But for the most part, in any recognised poetic scheme there is sufficient and frequent repetition of the same or of similar sounds, and it is, perhaps, here that we find our best clue to the underlying nature of poetic form.

The human mind has certain machine-like characteristics. One of these is that any experience tends to make, as it were, a channel down which other experiences may flow. If they do not, but insist on creating new routes for themselves, we are conscious of a certain difficulty; we feel that things go more easily, and with less effort, every time the original experience, or one closely similar, is repeated. That is true of practically every action. Every individual has grown accustomed to certain muscular movements in walking, and tends to go at the same pace, taking always the same length of stride. If, for any reason, it becomes necessary to quicken the pace or shorten the stride, there is a conscious effort which soon produces weariness. So in reading or hearing speech, we grow accustomed to certain series of sounds, and we pass over them easily and without conscious effort. It is far less difficult to recall them when we wish to do so. In other words, everything we have heard has created a certain *expectation* in our minds, and our satisfaction is to a large extent dependent on the way in which that expectation is fulfilled or unfulfilled.

It goes without saying that this is just as true of prose as it is of verse. Rhetorical writers like Cicero were careful to balance their clauses in sound as well as in sense, and it is this characteristic which, in no small measure, makes them acceptable authors. Whether we approve of the sentiments or not, most of us find an actual physical pleasure in listening to a passage of Macaulay, or of any other prose writer who has studied and cultivated the rhythm of his sentences, the aesthetic sequence of his vowels, and the harshness or smoothness of his consonantal sounds. But, in the nature of the case, the expectation created in a piece of prose is seldom completely fulfilled, or even nearly fulfilled. If it were, we should probably regard the fact as a blemish on the author's style, and he would certainly not deliberately repeat a series of sounds so soon after its first occurrence as to make us instantly recognise it. In poetry, on the other hand, we find that the expectation is always fulfilled, completely or nearly so ; if it were not we should have to deny the title of verse to any piece of writing, however magnificent it might be in other ways. *Vers libre*, it is true, breaks away from the strict sequence of sounds, and gives us an unfulfilled expectation, but it offers satisfaction of some other kind, in the simple cadence or in the parallelism of thought, if it be good verse. And some students of literature would deny that *vers libre* has the right to be called poetry, at least as far as its form is concerned.

On the other hand there must be some room for variation. An invariable sequence of sounds would give more than satisfaction, it would give satiety. The most rigid metres are probably those found in the lyric stanzas of Greek and Latin literature, and here we have considerable alternation of different feet within the stanza itself. The Sapphic verse, for example, consists of a series of iambus, spondee and dactyl ; in each of the first three lines the first two are repeated, as if the poet were attempting to reproduce the whole series and not quite succeeding. The fourth line, however, does give that completion, with an additional foot, as if the writer were triumphing over the fact that, after two failures, he had, at the third attempt, achieved the goal towards which he aimed. Here we have quite sufficient variation to avoid monotony and give pleasure ; moreover poems written in this and other lyric metres are commonly quite short.

In longer poems the relief from monotony may be obtained in two ways, often combined. One is the use of different feet (and a foot is only a definite series of sounds within a very limited space) as alternatives. The classical hexameter, for example, admits of either a dactyl or a spondee in any of the first four of the six feet. The amount of variation allowed in the iambic trimeter, the normal metre of dramatic dialogue, is comparatively small in Greek tragedy, though it is enough to escape monotony, but in later forms, as in Latin comedy, it is so great that the novice has considerable difficulty in scanning it at all. In modern verse, especially in English lyrics, we often meet with what is called *anacrusis*, when one or more syllables are prefixed to the metrical scheme proper in any line.

The other common method is that which is technically known as *enjambement*. This means that the sense unit and the verse unit do not coincide, but overlap, the grammatical sentence running on beyond the end of the poetic line into the next. The lines quoted earlier in this chapter from *Paradise Lost* and *In Memoriam* will serve as examples. Even if we were to insist on reading each poetic line or stanza for itself, our minds would inevitably be conscious of a certain incompleteness of thought, and we should make a break in the flow of our ideas at the end of a sentence, whether we would or not. In dramatic poetry this principle is sometimes carried so far that a line may be divided between two speakers. Thus in *The Tempest*, Act I, scene 2 we have the following :

PROSPERO : Awake, dear heart, awake, thou hast slept well ; Awake !

MIRANDA : The strangeness of your story put Heaviness in me.

PROSPERO : Shake it off. Come on, We'll visit Caliban, my slave, who never Yields us a kind answer.

MIRANDA : 'Tis a villain, sir, I do not love to look on.

PROSERO :   But as 'tis,
We cannot miss him : he does make our fire,
Fetch in our wood, and serves in offices
That profit us.   What ho ! slave : Caliban :
Thou earth, thou : speak.

CALIBAN (*Within*) :   There's wood enough within.

Here we have several clear cases of *enjambement* as between
the three speakers, and even where Prospero speaks more
than one line his sentences end in the middle of a verse.
We have other variations from the normal, also, which
help to give variety within uniformity.   " Heaviness "
is difficult to accent on the second syllable, as the strict
metre would require, and the Prospero-Miranda line :

" Yields us a kind answer.   'Tis a villain, sir."

has so to be read as to make two syllables take the place
of one ; we are almost tempted to leave out the first " a."
Here, then, we may find the characteristic feature of
poetic form, as distinct from that of prose.   It has several
advantages.   It arises in ages before writing becomes a
normal accomplishment, when few can even read what is
written.   Memory must play a large part in life, and the
mind needs a form which is comparatively easy to
memorize.   The predisposition created by one short
series of words, or even of sounds, demands that what
follows shall more or less correspond to it.   Most popular
proverbs have an assonance somewhere which serves
to protect them from being forgotten or badly mis-
rendered.   So arises the habit of putting memorable
thoughts into this form which not only creates expectation
but goes far towards satisfying it.   From this starting-
point we can proceed to glance at the characteristic type
of expectation which is produced and satisfied in Hebrew
verse.

II

THE FORMS OF HEBREW VERSE

As we have seen, the forms of poetry depend on the expectation aroused in the mind of a hearer or reader by a succession of units of speech. Poetry differs in form from prose in supplying a much more complete satisfaction to eye or ear ; in other words the succession tends to be regular, or at least symmetrical. This general principle may be applied to all forms of poetry, but there are wide differences in the means whereby the expectation is aroused and satisfied. In classical and in most modern poetry the units are *sounds*, and the poet may consider the length of his syllables, the comparative stress laid on them in speech, or vowel and consonant combinations at the beginning or end of the lines. In still older forms of poetry (e.g. in Accadian or Chinese) the unit is not a *sound* but an *idea*. It is the speaker's thought which rouses an expectation, and this can be satisfied only by a repetition or by a balancing conception. A word, or even a combination of words, may call up a mental picture, and the answer to it will of necessity be another picture. Where more than one word is involved, they must be capable of being so closely combined as to form a single concept in the mind of the hearer. What the new grammarians call " cement " words, in contrast to the " brick " words of noun and verb—words like prepositions, negative adverbs, and sometimes pronouns— are comparatively seldom so weighted with meaning as to form independent thought-units, and so they become parts of a larger whole.

It is to this general type of thought-rhythm that the forms of classical Hebrew poetry belong. Medieval writers, did, it is true, develop a kind of sound rhythm, based on the alternation of long and short syllables, the long being those which have a full vowel and the short those composed of a consonant with vocal Shewa. Such an arrangement, however, is, as far as we can judge, still unknown at the end of the Biblical period, and all our classical Hebrew poetry must be " scanned " on the older basis. Hence there arises a phenomenon to which the name " parallelism " was first given by Lowth in the middle of the eighteenth century.

The term is singularly apt. If we consider a piece of Hebrew narrative prose, we observe that it is normally a continuous stream of co-ordinate sentences linked together by conjunctions—in the Hebrew by " Waw Consecutives." It allows the thought of the reader, then, to pursue a straight and unbroken course. Even when we get syntactical and stylistic variations from the norm, they add something fresh to our thought. But when a statement is made in poetry, the expectation that has been roused in our minds must be satisfied as soon as possible ; a series of ideas has been put before us, and we instinctively require that it shall be repeated. So the poet goes back to the beginning again, and says the same thing once more, though he may partly or completely change the actual words in order to avoid monotony. He is, then, following a line of thought *parallel* to that which has been already laid down. We thus discover a fundamental principle of Hebrew verse form : *Every verse must consist of at least two " members," the second of which must, more or less completely, satisfy the expectation raised by the first.* A third member may be added ; where there are more than three, it is usually possible to group the members into twos and threes. It is impossible to exaggerate the importance of this principle in studying Hebrew verse forms. It means, for example, that there can be no such thing as a single verse-member ; the term " parallel " is as meaningless when applied to a single line of verse as it would be when similarly used in mathematics. A second corollary is that the terms of a verse-member stand in closer relation to one another than they do to any term in a preceding or in a following member. There can be no " syncopation " or " *enjambement* " in Hebrew poetry. If and when such a phenomenon appears to be present, closer examination will shew that the poet deliberately created a pause in the flow of his utterance, in order to keep the hearer for a moment in suspense, and so give added emphasis to what he was about to say. A recognition of this fact is of some importance in exegesis, as it often helps us to appreciate nuances in the writer's thought which would be missed by plain and straightforward translation.

Parallelism may take many forms. Lowth himself broadly recognized three. To the first he gave the name " synonymous," occurring when the theme is stated in the first member, and then re-stated with variation in the second. Thus in Ps. 1 : 5 we have :

Therefore the wicked shall not stand in the judgement,
Nor sinners in the congregation of the righteous.

where the second member is obviously only another way of saying the same thing as the first. Lowth's second form is " antithetic " parallelism, in which the second member states the truth of the first in a negative form or offers a contrast. Thus Ps. 1 : 6 runs :

For Yahweh knoweth the way of the righteous,
But the way of the wicked shall perish.

In a large number of instances, however, neither of these forms appears, and the sense runs directly on. So we find in Ps. 27 : 6 (first line) :

> But now shall my head be lifted up
> Above my enemies round about me.

For this sort of line Lowth used the term " synthetic " parallelism. It has, however, been generally recognized that, strictly speaking, it can hardly be called parallelism at all, and a much better name is that supplied by Buchanan Gray—" formal " parallelism.

Following the lines laid down by Lowth, later scholars identified three other types of parallelism (they may be seen in the introduction to Briggs' *Psalms*), " emblematic," " stairlike," and " introverted." The first term s applied in cases where the second member reproduces the thought of the first by means of a metaphor or simile. An example may be seen in Ps. 1 : 4 :

> The wicked are not so,
> But are like the chaff which the wind driveth away.

Another type may be seen in Ps. 103 : 13, where the love of God is illustrated by that of a human father. " Stairlike " parallelism may involve more than one line, and is to be recognized where one member (or part of a member) in one line is repeated in the second, and made the starting-point for a fresh step. An illustration may be taken from Ps. 29 : 1-2 :

> Ascribe to Yahweh,
> Ye sons of God,
> Ascribe to Yahweh
> Glory and strength ;
> Ascribe to Yahweh
> The glory of his name,
> Bow before Yahweh
> In holy splendour.

In the first three lines we are mounting, as it were, step by step to the climax in v. 2. Each line both carries us back to the starting-point and gives us a new item from which we may make further progress. The last type also involves at least two complete lines, and is applied in cases where the first member of one line corresponds to the second member of the first, and the second member of the first to the first member of the second, a chiastic arrangement which may be represented as a.b.b.a. Briggs quotes Ps. 30 : 8-10 as an example :

Unto thee, O Yahweh, do I cry ; and unto the Lord do I make
    supplication :
    What profit is there in my blood when I go down to the pit ?
    Shall the dust praise thee ? Shall it declare thy truth ?
Hear, O Yahweh, and be gracious to me ; be thou my helper.

Lowth's position has never been seriously challenged, except in so far as his third type of parallelism has been recognized as not being true parallelism at all. All later students of Hebrew prosody have at least paid lip service to his principles, though during the last sixty or seventy years there has been a tendency to overlook their implications. It is, perhaps, natural that when dealing with a language like Hebrew no clear distinction should be drawn between a " logical " and a " phonetic " arrangement. The accent in Hebrew is so strong that it largely controls the accidence of the language, and it seems as if the whole force and meaning of a word were summed up and concentrated in the stressed syllable, which may be the penult, though it is more commonly the last. Reading Hebrew poetry, with due attention to the accent and to parallelism, certainly gives the impression of an accentual rhythm, though there seems to be no rule as to the proportion or relation between the accented and the unaccented syllables. It is impossible to deny alto-

gether the influence of the sound of words as distinct
from their meaning, but the essential principle of parallelism requires that sound should be very much subordinate
to sense.

It is not, then, surprising that since the seventies of the
last century, scholars should have concentrated on the
" stresses " or " beats " in their efforts to analyse the
verse-member into its component parts. Valuable con-
tributions have been made to the study of Hebrew
phonetics in general, but, as a rule, these apply as much
to words used in prose as to poetry. One great scholar
(Sievers), for example, believed that the normal Hebrew
" foot " was an accentual anapaest. But his anapaest
admitted more than two unaccented syllables preceding
the accent, and even one such syllable after the main
stress. This, of course, is simply a phonetic description
of any normal Hebrew word. Scholars believed that
Hebrew should be scanned by the enumeration of
" stresses " in each verse-member. A difficulty was
created by the fact that in a number of instances it seemed
that a word must have two " stresses " in order to produce
anything like metrical regularity, and a great deal of
patient study and research has been devoted to solving
the problem of the phonetic conditions in which a word
could be doubly stressed. The value of these studies for
the specific subject of Hebrew verse form lies in the
analysis of the verse-member into its component units.
This is equally valid, whether those units indicate sound
or thought, and in the work of the late Buchanan Gray
we had for the first time a return to, and a real development of, the principles laid down by Lowth. It is still
usual to speak of " stresses " or " beats " in describing
Hebrew verse forms, but since these terms may be mis-
leading, the word " unit " will be employed to indicate

the smallest recognizable element in a Hebrew poetic line.

Parallelism in its simplest form requires that every unit in the first member of a verse should be exactly balanced by a unit in the second member. So Ps. 103 : 3 runs :

> Who-forgiveth all thine-iniquities ;
> Who-healeth all thy-diseases.

(Hyphened words represent single words or single thought-units in Hebrew.) This may be represented by the formula :

> a. b. c.
> a'. b'. c'.

But it is comparatively seldom that we meet with so exact a correspondence between the members of a verse ; indeed if such a form were normal the monotony would become almost intolerable. It is to Buchanan Gray that we owe the soundest attempt to analyse and classify the various forms that parallelism may take. He distinguished between *complete parallelism*, of which the verse just cited forms an example, and *incomplete parallelism*, in which the units of the second member do not correspond exactly to those of the first. Here again there is an important division. In some lines we may have the same number of units in both parts, though one or more in the second may not balance units in the first. To this type Gray gave the name *incomplete parallelism with compensation*. In other cases there is one unit less in one member than in the other (usually the second is the shorter), and for these Gray used the phrase *incomplete parallelism without compensation*. Ps. 103 : 15 offers an example of the former type :

> As-for-man his-days are-as-grass ;
>   as-a-flower-of the-field so-he-flourisheth.

This may be represented :

                a. b. c.
                c'. d. e.

though it is to be noted that in the second member two units (as-a-flower-of the-field) correspond to a single unit in the first member.   This is a very common form of compensation, e.g. in v. 7 of the same Psalm we have :

He-made-known his-ways unto-Moses,
                To-the-children-of Israel his-acts.

Here the first two units of the second member correspond in sense to the third unit of the first member ; we may represent the form as :

                a. b. c.
                c'. c'. b'.

The possible variations of incomplete parallelism with compensation are almost unlimited, and an observation oı its forms will contribute in no small degree to an appreciation of the beauty of Hebrew poetry.

Incomplete parallelism without compensation produces lines which often give the impression of an echo.   It was this type of line which attracted the attention of Budde to the possibility of " metre " in Hebrew poetry, and to it he gave the name *Qinah*, because he first identified it in *Lamentations*, and believed it to be characteristic of the dirge.   Indeed, it was not until the last years of his life that he was prepared to recognize any other form in Hebrew prosody.   A good example may be found in Lam. 3 : 4 :

He-hath-worn-out my-flesh and-my-skin,
He-hath-broken my-bones.

This may be represented by the formula :

                a. b. c.
                a'. b'.

A more obvious illustration of the same type is to be seen in Is. 40 : 4 (second line) :

> And-the-crooked shall-be-made straight,
> And-the-rough-places   plain.

(In the Hebrew the verb stands first in the sentence.) V. 2 of the same chapter gives an example of a line in which the second unit in the first-member has no parallel in the second :

> Speak-ye comfortably to-Jerusalem,
> And-cry   unto-her.

This is of the form

> a. b. c.
> a'.   c'.

Cases in which the third unit is left without a parallel are much less frequent than the other two. They do, however, occur, as in the second line of Lam. 2 : 10 :

> They-have-cast-up dust upon-their-heads ;
> They-have-girded-themselves with-sackcloth.

This may be represented as

> a. b. c.
> a'. b'.

It may be remarked that, perhaps not unnaturally, we shall find in lines of this type far more instances of " formal " parallelism than in those whose members are of equal length.

The types of parallelism which we have noted so far are mainly examples of the balance of two members of the same line. Very often, however, we find two lines standing closely together and shewing a balance between whole lines, and not merely between the parts of the same line. The former type we may call *internal parallelism*, the latter *external parallelism*. As might be expected, complete external parallelism is comparatively rare, but cases do occur, as in Is. 1 : 10 :

Hear the-word-of the-Lord,   ye-rulers-of Sodom ;
Giver-ear-unto the-law-of our-God, ye-people-of Gomorrah.

This is clearly

     a. b. c.   d. e.
     a'. b'. c'.   d'. e'.

Normally, however, external parallelism is incomplete with compensation. It may be very nearly complete, as in Ps. 27 : 1 :

The-Lord is-my-light and-my-salvation ;
    whom shall-I-fear ?
The-Lord is-the-strength-of my-life ;
    of-whom shall-I-be-afraid ?

Here the parallel between the two second members is complete, while as between the two first members it is incomplete with compensation, taking that common form in which two units in one member balance a single unit in the other. In other cases the order may, so to speak, be inverted (Briggs' " introverted " parallelism), as in the second and third lines of Lam. 1 : 1 :

She-is-become as-a-widow,   she-that-was-great among-
     nations ;
Princess among-provinces,   she-is-become tributary.

This is of the form :

     a. b.   c. d.
     c'. d'.   a'. b'.

To the same general class belong those cases in which part of a line is paralleled or even repeated, and the remainder carries the thought still further—" stairlike " parallelism. So Ps. 27 : 2 runs (A.V. has inverted two members) :

When-the-wicked came upon-me,   to-eat-up my-flesh.
Mine-enemies and-my-foes,   they stumbled and-fell,

Here the first member of the second line takes up one unit from the first line, and then completes the sentence left imperfect in the first line.

It is impossible to go further into detail in describing the forms which parallelism may take. It is enough to call attention to the facts, and the reader must be left to apply the principles suggested to each poem, indeed to each line. Only so will the full beauty of Hebrew verse form be realized, with its general uniformity and its almost infinite variety within the limits necessarily imposed on the poet by the conditions of his language and his thought.

We must now turn to the various ways in which units may be combined to form verse-members and so lines. It is clear that two units is the minimum required for a verse-member. And the facts show that it is very rare, if, indeed, it ever happens, that a verse-member should contain more than three units. In all the examples hitherto quoted it will be observed that every member contains either two or three units, and it seems clear that all Hebrew " metres " are combinations of twos and threes. Where we have more than two units it is practically always possible still further to subdivide ; a " 4 " can normally be read as " 2 : 2 " and a " 5 " as " 3 : 2 " or (more rarely) " 2 : 3." It is, then, a very simple matter to find names for the various metres ; they are always indicated merely by the number of units in each member.

The shortest " metre," then, will be the 2 : 2. It is not uncommon in the Psalms, and its quick, staccato movement often indicates a high emotional tension, sometimes due to fear or awe, and sometimes to exuberant happiness. Ps. 29 is almost pure 2 : 2, and the reader can feel the nervous strain imposed by the successive crashes of violent thunder. The metrical structure is, unfortunately, often obscured in our familiar translations, but we can catch something of the emotional tone even through the English of v. 5 :

| The-voice-of the-Lord | breaketh the-cedars ; |
| Yea-the-Lord breaketh | the-cedars-of Lebanon. |

(Note the external stairlike parallelism.)   The opposite feeling-tone is expressed in Ps. 46, which, again, is almost pure 2 : 2.   So v. 2 :

Therefore will-not-we-fear,   though-the-earth be-removed,
And-though-the-mountains be-carried
                                into-the-midst-of the-sea.
Or v. 6 :

| The-heathen raged, | the-kingdoms were-moved; |
| He-uttered his-voice, | the-earth melted. |

One of the commonest metres in the Bible is the 3 : 2. Its parallelism is often merely formal, though the regular forms are quite frequent.   In Ps. 27 : 4, for example, we have :

One-thing have-I-desired of-the-Lord,   that will-I-seek-after;
That-I-may-dwell in-the-house-of the-Lord   all-the-days-of
                                                my-life,
To-behold the-beauty-of the-Lord,   and-to-enquire in-his-
                                                temple.

Here the parallelism is somewhat intricate.   There is incomplete parallelism in the first line.   In a sense the second line is parallel to the whole of the first, since it expands the " that " of the second member.   In itself this second line offers only formal parallelism.   The third line presents internal incomplete parallelism, and, even so, the last unit of the second member does not corres-pond exactly to any unit in the first.   As a metre, the 3 : 2 is slower and more dignified than the 2 : 2, and, as has been remarked, it is often used in dirges.

There are instances where it seems as if a five-unit line should be divided as 2 : 3, and not as 3 : 2. Thus in Is. 40 : 4 we read :

Every-valley shall-be-exalted, and-every-mountain and-hill
    shall-be-made-low.

Here the sense certainly seems to demand that the break (often called, in imitation of classical prosody, a " caesura ") shall come where the comma is placed. But sometimes there may be another explanation. So Ps. 28 : 6, normally read, would have to be arranged :

Blessed-be the-Lord,
    Because-he-hath-heard the-voice-of my-supplication.

But suppose we read it :

Blessed-be the-Lord, because-he-hath-heard
    The-voice-of my-supplication.

The first member is obviously incomplete, and creates in us a strong expectation of an object to follow the verb. But there is a break in the flow of thought, and we are held, as it were, in suspense. The effect is to emphasize and drive home the force both of the verb and of its object, and it may quite well have been the intention of the poet thus to enhance our sense of the benefit he has received : " he has heard—yes, he has heard the voice of my supplication." A number of apparent cases of 2 : 3 can thus be reduced to 3 : 2 with advantage to the reader, but there still remain instances where this is hardly probable, and we are forced to admit the possibility of a 2 : 3, though the general tendency in Hebrew verse is to place the longer member first.

Another large group of poems has the metrical form 3 : 3. This is, indeed, the most frequent metre in Biblical poetry. The whole of the poem of Job is written in it, and it is the commonest metre in the Psalter. Internal

parallelism is normal, and it is often complete. An
instance from Ps. 103 has already been quoted (p. 26),
and there are many others. More often the parallelism
is incomplete, naturally with compensation. So Ps.
24 : 1 :

> The-Lord's is-the-earth and-the-fulness-thereof,
> The-world and-they-that-dwell therein.

For this the formula would be :

> a. b. c.
> b'. c'. d'.

but it is to be noted that in sense the last two units of the
second member balance the third unit of the first member.
We may take a couple of lines from Job 4 : 17f. :

> Shall-mortal-man be-more-just than-God,
> Shall-a-man be-more-pure than-his-maker ?
> Behold, he-put-no-trust in-his-servants,
> And-his-angels he-charged with-folly.

Here the parallelism in the first line is complete, though in
the Hebrew text the order of the terms is not the same in
the two members, while in the second it is incomplete
with compensation, since there is nothing in the second
member to correspond to " Behold," and the second and
third units of the second member taken together correspond to the third (in the Hebrew order) unit of the first.
We may note, too, that this is what Lowth would call
" antithetic " parallelism, since the first member states
the idea negatively, the second positively.

We find from time to time that with the 3 : 3 we have a
third member, giving 3 : 3 : 3. This sometimes occurs
in poems which are normally 3 : 3, as in Ps. 103 : 20 :

> Bless the-Lord, ye-his-angels
> That-excel-in-strength, that-do his-commandments,
> Hearkening unto-the-voice-of his-word.

B

In these cases many scholars are inclined to suspect that one of the three members is a later insertion, due to textual corruption, and it is a remarkable fact that in Job, where they are fairly frequent, there are often grounds for suspecting the originality of one of three members, entirely apart from metrical considerations ; one, for instance, is often not represented in the text of the LXX. But there remain enough to give ground for the belief that this form does occur in 3 : 3 poems. A few pieces are almost entirely composed of 3 : 3 : 3. So the last part of Ps. 24, beginning with v. 7, runs :

> Lift-up your-heads, O-ye-gates,
>> And-be-ye-lift-up ye-everlasting doors,
>> And-the-king-of glory shall-come-in.

In cases of this kind, two of the three members are as a rule more closely parallel to one another than to the third, as here, but there are instances in which all three seem to be equally closely related. An example may be taken from Ps. 100 : 1f. :

> Make-a-joyful-noise unto-the-Lord all-the-earth,
>> Serve the-Lord with-gladness,
>> Come before-his-presence with-singing.

Here the parallels are not exact—they may be generally described as being incomplete with compensation, but all are equally allied in sense.

While dealing with this triplication of members, we may note the fact that a form 2 : 2 : 2 is sometimes found. It is quite characteristic of prophetic poetry, but is comparatively rare elsewhere. A good instance occurs in Ps. 91 : 3 :

> Surely-he shall-deliver-thee
>> From-the-snare-of the-fowler,
>>> And from-the-noisome pestilence.

Here the second and third members are closely parallel, while both complete the thought of the first. Another example, in which all three members are parallel, may be seen in Job 17 : 1 :

> My-breath is-corrupt,
>   My-days are-extinct,
>   The-graves are-ready-for-me.

But this arrangement occurs so seldom in the strictly " poetical " books that we might hesitate to admit it were it not for its frequent appearance in the Prophets.

A 4 : 3 undoubtedly exists, though it is far from common. It may be further subdivided, and described as a 2 : 2 : 3, though, as a rule, the second member is more closely linked with the first than with the third. Indeed, in its normal form, the third is parallel to the first two together. It is uncommon in the Psalms, though Ps. 141 may offer an example. The first part of v. 4 runs :

> Incline-not my-heart   to-any-evil thing,
>   To-practise wicked works.

And the previous verse :

> Set, O-Lord,   a-watch before-my-mouth,
>   Keep the-door-of my-lips.

As an illustration from Proverbs we may take 20 : 2 :

> The-fear-of a-king   is-as-the-roaring-of a-lion,
>   Whoso-provoketh-him-to-anger sinneth-against his-own-
>   soul.

This offers the characteristic parallelism. But the finest example in the Bible is the great vision of " chaos come again " in Jer. 4 : 23-26. The first two verses run :

> I-beheld the-earth,   and-lo, it-was-without-form-and-void ;
>   And-the-heavens and-they-had-no light.
> I-beheld the-mountains, and-lo, they-trembled ;
>   And-all the-hills moved-lightly.

It is even possible that there are instances of 3 : 4, but they must be so rare as to be practically negligible.

Before we pass on to consider the use made by poets of these various " metres " in constructing their pieces, mention should be made of one other phenomenon. That is " anacrusis," a name given to a unit standing at the beginning of a line, which is not counted in its enumeration. From time to time we meet with cases where the initial word clearly stands alone, and it is the second word in the verse with which the metre proper starts. Such words are usually comparatively small— interjections, conjunctions, or pronouns. They have a special function in the flow of the verse, for they produce a pause, and, by making the reader halt, call attention to and emphasize what follows. A good instance may be seen in the opening verses of chs. 1, 2 and 4 in *Lamentations*. The word rendered " How " is not an interrogative ; it does not even ask a rhetorical question. It is an exclamation, almost a groan. This becomes clear when we look at such lines as the first two of Lam. 1 : 1 (some changes in the EVV. are inevitable) :

Oh !
   The-city doth-sit solitary   that-was-full-of people ;
   She-has-become as-a-widow   that-was-great among-
                                        nations.

Obviously the parallelism requires this arrangement of the second member of each line, and that would leave four units to the first half of the first line—an abnormal arrangement. And it will hardly be doubted that the verse gains in intensity as the note of utter woe is struck even before the poem proper begins. An example of a pronoun most effectively used in this way comes from Ps. 3 : 3. The Psalmist has just stated the substance of his complaint, and has called attention to the enemies who threaten and mock him. Then he turns to God, and marks the changed address thus :

But thou—
    Thou-O-Lord art-a-shield for-me
                my-glory and-the-lifter-up-of my-head.

We note the same phenomenon in Job 3 : 20 :

Why, oh why
    Is-light given to-him-that-is-in-misery,
             and-life unto-the-bitter-in soul ?

Here the first word (rendered " wherefore" in the EVV.) introduces a rhetorical question, but the parallelism and the number of units alike suggest that it should be treated apart from the line itself, and again the pause makes what follows extremely impressive.

We now turn to a question on which there is still no general agreement. Is the same metre always used throughout a poem, or did the Hebrew poets vary their metres ? It may be admitted at once that it is impossible to obtain a regular metre in most of our Biblical pieces without resorting to emendation. Not infrequently, it is true, the required modification is indicated by the text of the LXX or on other grounds, but when allowance has been made for these, there still remain numbers of passages in which the metre varies. Indeed, there seems to be hardly a poem in the whole Bible in which the metre indicated by the Massoretic text is absolutely regular. At the same time, there is evidence to suggest that originally a certain measure of uniformity was maintained. In addition to the facts provided by the LXX and other ancient versions, we have in the Bible a few cases of passages which appear in several places. Thus Pss. 14 and 53 are nearly identical, and one of the best known of prophetic utterances occurs both in Isaiah 2 and in Micah 4. More than once in the passages

a verse which is " irregular " in one form is " regular "
in the other. We have good reason to believe that many
of our Psalms had a long history, and may well have
suffered modification which destroyed complete metrical
regularity. But even when allowance is made for all
these facts, we still have a very large number of " irregular " lines in the Psalter and elsewhere.

When we come, however, to consider these irregular-
ities in detail, we find that the great majority fall into
clearly marked classes. Thus in 3 : 3 poems (especially
in the Prophets) we find at times lines which can be
described only as 2 : 2 : 2. It is very rarely that we meet
with an unmixed 3 : 2 ; nearly always there will be
some lines which can be nothing but 2 : 2. It is interesting to observe that this sometimes occurs where the
emotional tension is obviously rising. An excellent
example is supplied by Ps. 23 :

The-Lord-is my-shepherd, I-shall-not-want ;
    he-maketh-me-to-lie-down in-green-pastures.   3 : 2
He-leadeth-me beside-the-still waters,
                he-restoreth my-soul.   3 : 2
He-leadeth-me in-the-paths-of righteousness
                  for-his-name's sake.   3 : 2
Yes-though I-walk   through-the-valley-of the-shadow-
                      of-death,   2 : 2
I-will-fear-no evil   for-thou-art with-me.   2 : 2
Thy-rod and-thy-staff   they comfort-me.   2 : 2
Thou-preparest a-table before-me
             in-the-presence-of mine-enemies ;   3 : 2
Thou-anointest my-head with-oil,
                my-cup runneth-over.   3 : 2
Surely-goodness and-mercy shall-follow-me
              all-the-days-of my-life.   3 : 2
And-I-will-dwell in-the-house-of the-Lord   for ever.   3 : 2

Sometimes, though very rarely, it becomes necessary to
divide a five-unit line into 2 : 3 rather than 3 : 2.

This alternation of fours and fives is so common as to constitute a regular variation, and its presence is not to be held as an indication of a real change in the metre. On the other hand, the appearance of a four- or five-unit line in the middle of 3 : 3 is sufficiently uncommon to awaken our doubts as to the accuracy of the text as it has been transmitted to us. So also we may suspect the presence of a 3 : 3 line in a poem which is mainly 3 : 2 and 2 : 2.

There are thus two main metrical forms. In the one we have 3 : 3, sometimes varied with 2 : 2 : 2 and 3 : 3 : 3 —the commoner of the two ; and in the other 3 : 2 varied with 2 : 2 and occasionally with 2 : 3. The 4 : 3 is so rare in continuous poems that it is impossible to note any " regular " variation.

At this point it will be convenient to mention the use of an acrostic in a small number of Hebrew poems, though it is far from being a regular feature of Hebrew verse-form. This is an arrangement in which each verse or group of lines is characterized by having a particular letter at the beginning, the letters being arranged in alphabetical order. We may illustrate the principle by trying to render the opening verses of Ps. 34 (an acrostic poem in Hebrew)—with some periphrasis— :

A   At all times I will bless the Lord,
     His praise shall be continually in my mouth.
B   Boasteth my soul in the Lord,
     The humble shall hear thereof and be glad.
C   Call the Lord great with me,
     And let us exalt his name together.
D   Did I seek the Lord ? then he heard me,
     And delivered me from all my fears.
E   Every man that looked to him was lightened,
     And their faces were not ashamed.
F   For this poor man cried and the Lord heard him,
     And saved him out of all his troubles.

Such poems often have thus a single line to each letter, but this is far from being an invariable rule. Thus Pss. 111, 112 have half a line only—something like :

A   All my heart shall praise the Lord,
B   Being in the assembly of the upright and the congregation.
C   Countless are the works of the Lord,
D   Desiring them, all men seek them.

In other instances more than one line belongs to each letter. Pss. 9-10 (originally one) and Lam. 4 are arranged in pairs of lines, the first of which begins with the appropriate letter. Lam. 1 and 2 have three lines to each group, and, again, the acrostic is marked only in the first of the three. In one or two cases the poet has gone further, and has given a group of lines each of which begins with the proper letter. Lam. 3 is arranged in sections of three lines each—

A   Affliction have I seen
        By the rod of his wrath.
A   As he led me, he brought me
        Into darkness and not into light.
A   Against me indeed is he turned, he turneth
        His hand against me all the day.
B   By age hath he worn my flesh and my skin,
        He hath broken my bones.
B   Barriers hath he built against me, and compassed me
        With gall and travail.
B   Between dark places hath he set me,
        As they that be dead of old.
C   Confining walls about me hath he made, that I cannot get out.
        He hath made heavy my chains.
C   Cry I also and shout ?
        He shutteth out my prayer.
C   Closely hath he shut in my ways with hewn stone,
        He hath made my paths crooked.

The outstanding poem of this type is Ps. 119, which is arranged in groups of no less than eight lines, each of which begins with its appropriate letter. A poet writing in acrostic must sometimes have found his scheme difficult, but this class includes some of the most moving pieces we have, e.g., Lam. 1-4.

We have now to consider the combination of lines to form larger groups. It is, of course, possible to divide any but the shortest poems into verse paragraphs, and, indeed, this must be done if a piece is to be understood properly. But it does not follow that such an arrangement is strictly an element in the poetic form. *Paradise Lost* must be thus treated, but no one would maintain that these divisions form a part of the structure of English blank verse. We shall necessarily require a certain regularity, if not uniformity, in the number of lines in each group, and, in Hebrew poetry at any rate, the prosody-group must coincide with the sense-group, i.e., the divisions in the poem must be identical with the divisions in the thought. Yet for over a century it has been widely recognized that such larger groups are to be found in Hebrew poetry, and were an element in the technique of the poet. Since the earlier investigators were still largely dominated by the conceptions proper to classical poetry, the Greek name " strophe " (properly applying only to certain types of lyric verse) was used, and has never been wholly superseded, though we shall understand the character and function of these divisions better if we use the term " stanza."

As first propounded, the theory took into account the number of verses in the Massoretic text of each piece. Later it was realized that this arrangement did not always correspond to the original arrangement contemplated by the poet, and students counted the actual lines in each stanza. In both cases a fairly wide latitude was allowed. Generally speaking, four types of stanza arrangement were admitted. In the first all the stanzas in a poem had the same number of lines, and there are commentaries on the Psalter which assume that this is the only possible arrangement. Others, however, admitted that a series of stanzas, with different numbers of lines, might be repeated ; thus the first stanza might have three lines, the second four, the third five, the fourth three, the fifth four and the sixth five, the series 3, 4, 5 being continued throughout the piece. Or the series, instead of being exactly repeated, might be inverted—3, 4, 5, 5, 4, 3. In such cases an odd stanza might be inserted to mark the middle, sometimes consisting of a single line— 3, 4, 5, 1, 5, 4, 3. There were even poems in which no regular arrangement could be detected, and, following the Greek terminology, such poems were called " dithyrambic." It is difficult to see how a stanza arrangement of the last type can really be regarded as an element in poetic form.

While most modern scholars accept a stanza theory in Hebrew poetry, the attempt to reduce all Old Testament verse to such a form almost invariably leads to considerable interference with the text. No doubt many additions and corruptions have crept in during the long history of transmission. Especially in the Psalms, successive ages have modified the poet's language to suit their own needs and particular views, but, in the absence of direct textual evidence, either from ancient Hebrew copies or from still older versions, there must always remain a greater or lesser element of insecurity about alterations based on a metrical theory. We need stronger grounds than those frequently offered before we can be reasonably satisfied that a particular poem has been subjected to the very large amount of modification which a strict stanza theory often requires. Thus Ps. 23 contains, as it stands, ten lines. The natural grouping is 2, 4, 4—the shepherd, the guide and the host. Even if we take the second line of v. 3 with the preceding instead of the following words, we still have the irregularity 3, 3, 4. To meet this difficulty and to secure regularity, one modern commentator assumes that a whole line has dropped out in v. 4, while another regards the words " for thou art " as a later insertion in v. 4, at the same time adopting a very awkward metrical arrangement. Even a superficial study of recent scholarly works on the Psalms shews that we are often compelled either to abandon the theory of a uniform stanza structure or to resort to drastic surgery of the text.

At the same time, the stanza form is often unmistakable. It is obvious, for example, in Lam. 1, 2 and 4, where it is attested by the acrostic form of the poems. The same remark may be made about Ps. 119, where the poet seems to have tried to introduce eight different terms for the Law into each of his eight-line stanzas. It does not, however, follow that this kind of acrostic necessarily involves stanza structure, for there are instances in Lam. 3 where the sense seems to run on from one letter to the next without a serious break. Further, most of the acrostic poems in the Bible have only one line to each letter.

It may generally be assumed that a refrain indicates stanza form. Even here it may be necessary to suspect the accuracy of the text, since unequal groups of lines may appear. One of the best examples is to be seen in Pss. 42-43 (originally a single Psalm), where we have the same couplet in 42 : 5, 11 ; 43 : 5 (the apparent variation in 42 : 5 is certainly due to textual error). But the first " stanza " contains nine lines, the second ten and the third eight. Is it too much to suspect that a line has been accidentally transposed from the third stanza to the second ? The second line of 42 : 10, for example, would not be seriously out of place between 43 : 1 and 2. Ps. 46 offers an interesting example of a refrain. The same words occur in vv. 7 and 11, and this suggests that at one time they also found a place after v. 3. As our text now stands, v. 3 ends with the mysterious " Selah," which occurs also after the refrain in vv. 7 and 11. It appears that the refrain was added at a comparatively late stage in the history of the poem, for it contains the divine name Yahweh, elsewhere avoided in this part of the Psalter (Its presence in the Massoretic text of v. 8 is almost certainly due to textual corruption). But the general character of the piece leads us to believe that it did originally consist of three well-marked stanzas, each containing six 2 : 2 lines. It is true that the maintenance of this form requires several conjectural emendations, and, therefore, we may not dogmatize as to the primitive arrangement, but the necessary alterations commend themselves on other grounds than those of metre.

The term " Selah," again, is often held to indicate a stanza structure. Unfortunately its meaning is quite obscure, and had evidently been forgotten even by the time that the Greek version was made. The consonants are usually referred to a root meaning " uplift," and this is explained either as a heightening of the accompaniment, or, on the other hand, the cessation of instrumental music. Other possibilities are that it indicates a louder tone or a pause, or the insertion of a doxology or other refrain. The whole question, however, is quite uncertain. The vowels, as they stand in the Hebrew text, are incompatible with the root cited, but may be explained as implying

that another term was to be used. But the root itself
appears elsewhere in words which do not simply mean
" uplift," but " pile up," and both the main verb and its
derivatives are commonly used of erecting a mound of
earth, either as a siege process or to form a causeway for a
road. We can hardly regard this explanation of the term
as satisfactory, but no other seems any better.

Further difficulties in the way of seeing in this form a
metrical indication are raised by the fact that it occurs
in little more than a quarter of the Psalms, and elsewhere only in Hab. 3. Sometimes, as in Ps. 46, it does
stand at the ends of fairly equal divisions of a poem, but
in other cases it quite fails to suggest anything like an
even grouping of the lines. Much of this, however,
may be due to textual corruption, since the evidence of
the ancient versions does not always support the distribution of the term in the Massoretic text, and we cannot
exclude the possibility that it was intended originally to
mark the close of a regular stanza.

Finally we may observe that a stanza division may
sometimes be indicated simply by natural sense-groups.
This, indeed, is a *sine qua non*, whatever other criterion
may appear. Naturally different readers may feel that
a poem should be differently divided ; it is often not
clear whether a line goes closely with what precedes or
with what follows. In such cases the stanza arrangement,
if rendered probable by the rest of the poem, may serve
as a useful guide, and be of real value in exegesis. Ps. 91,
for example, clearly falls into eight two-line stanzas,
each of which is compact in itself, and shews a certain
independence of its neighbours. We cannot help seeing
the intimate connexion between vv. 3 and 4, 5 and 6,
11 and 12. Other pairs are quite natural, but the link
between vv. 13 and 14 might not have occurred to us

unless we had other evidence as to the structure of the poem. In view of that structure, however, we may be certain that these two verses are to be taken closely together, and any sound exegesis of them will be based on that fact. After all, it is sound exegesis which should be the final aim of all other branches of Biblical study.

III

ISOLATED POEMS

In trying to classify the types of poem which have been preserved in the Old Testament, we are faced with much the same kind of difficulty as that which we had to meet in considering poetic form. We are accustomed to thinking in the categories of Greek and Latin poetry ; we may refer also to other literatures, e.g. to Sanskrit. We are tempted to look for dramatic, epic, and lyric verse, and to assume that each will have the general characteristics which appear in the Classics. But it is doubtful whether any dramatic poetry has survived, if it ever existed in Israel, and we certainly have no epic, if by that we understand a narrative poem of some length. Only one extensive poem has come down to us, that of the Book of Job. This describes spiritual progress and mental experience, with no incident till the end is reached, for the narratives at the beginning and end of the book are in prose, not in poetry. Judged by classical standards, the only type of poetry we can find with certainty is the lyric. Even the book of Job may be regarded as a series of lyrics, though these are so closely connected as to form a single consecutive whole.

We may, nevertheless, distinguish several types of poetry in what has come down to us. There is some evidence to suggest that the ancient Hebrews themselves were conscious of these differences, and made collections of poems dealing with the same or parallel themes. In Num. 21 : 14, for example, mention is made of " The

Book of the Wars of Yahweh," which was, presumably, a collection of victory odes. Then, again, Josh. 10 : 13 and II Sam. 1 : 18 speak of a " Book of Yashar," a title which leaves room for discussion. The term literally means " upright," and it seems that the two poems referred to it are that which commemorated Joshua's victory at Beth-horon and " The Song of the Bow," which may or may not have been David's dirge over Saul and Jonathan. There is little here to indicate the general character of this collection. " Yashar " may be a shortened form—shortened by accident or design—of the name " Israel," which would leave room for a wide range of subjects. It may even be a corruption of the familiar word " *shir* " (the only change is the transposition of the first two letters), which means simply " song." If this suggestion is correct, there is even less guidance as to the definite type to which the collected poems were assigned by the compilers. All we can say for certain is that at one period in Israel's literary history (and that probably pre-exilic), collections of poems were known and used.

The existence of these collections is known to us from the fact that poems included in them are quoted in our Bibles. Apart from the prophetic books and the formal poetic collections, nearly fifty poems of various kinds have been embedded in the prose of the Pentateuch and the historical books. Some of these are very ancient, and may have been handed down from what we may call pre-Israelite times ; others are hymns and similar compositions which belong to a comparatively late period. Often we have reason to suspect that a piece had undergone more or less serious mutilation before it was placed in its present position, and in the case of the older poems we frequently have to allow for the possibility of some modification in the course of a long history. It may be remarked in passing that a few general poems have come down to us in the prophetic books as well as in the prose books proper, but these lie outside the range of our present studies.

The poems thus preserved in the books Genesis to II Kings seem to fall into five groups. These are :

1. Tribal and local songs.
2. Spells (curses and blessings).
3. *Meshalim.*
4. Paeans.
5. Dirges.

The division is not exact, and some poems may well be assigned to more than one of these groups. The third, in particular, is very difficult to define, and many of the pieces included in it might well be classed otherwise if they were not expressly described as *meshalim*. But we may accept the arrangement as roughly serviceable, and consider very briefly the individual poems coming under each head. Fuller treatment will be found in the various commentaries on the books in which the poems appear.

1. *Tribal and local songs*

Some of these may well be classed as spells, while certain poems included under the latter head might be described as tribal. There are, however, four pieces in which the tribal or local element seems to predominate. They commemorate some event or characteristic in the history of a tribe or of a place.

(i) Gen. 4 : 23f. The Song of Lamech. Metre, apparently, 3 : 2. The tribe of Lamech commemorates its extreme vindictiveness. The Cainites were famous for demanding seven lives for every one of their own ; Lamechites require seventy-seven.

(ii) Num. 21 : 14f. A badly mutilated and probably corrupt fragment. It begins with the object of an absent verb, and beyond the fact that it seems to celebrate some event in the distant past which took place to the east of the Jordan, it is difficult to make any definite assertion about it.

(iii) Num. 21 : 17f. The Song of the Well. Metre 3 : 2 (2 : 2). This might be regarded as a spell, but in its setting it has a special local reference. It was, very probably, a formula used by any well-diggers in ancient Israel, and, like the last, very likely goes back to the age preceding the Israelite conquest of Palestine.

(iv) Num. 21 : 27-30. The Song of Heshbon and Moab. Metre uncertain though perhaps originally 3 : 3. We have here apparently a record of the conquest by Sihon of the debatable territory lying between the Arnon and the Jabbok. In the monarchical period this was claimed by both Israel and Moab, and occupied by each in turn. The song here preserved seems to form a part of Israel's " title " ; the claim is that since Sihon annexed the land in question, destroying the power of Moab, Israel, by conquering Sihon, established a right to occupy all the country he had acquired.

2. *Spells*

There is a wide-spread belief in the practical efficiency of the spoken word. When a person, temporarily or permanently endowed with abnormal power, utters a word indicating prosperity or calamity, that word in itself brings about the result which it foretells. Its power lies partly in the authority of the person speaking and partly in the form which the utterance takes. People like prophets and wizards have this capacity for controlling the future at all times, if they choose to throw their language into the proper form ; even ordinary men may become " fey " in special circumstances. In particular the last utterances of a dying man may have peculiarly effective force ; hence the desire to procure a death-bed blessing which so often appears in the older literature of many peoples. Some seventeen poems in the prose books may be grouped under this head, though several of them might also be included in other classes.

(i) Gen. 9 : 25, 26f. The blessing and curse of Noah. Metre 3 : 3 (2 : 2 : 2). Canaan is cursed while Japhet and Shem are blessed. The saying is probably very ancient, and explains certain ethnological and political relationships to which we have lost the clue.

(ii) Gen. 14 : 19b-20a. Melchizedek's blessing of Abraham. Metre 3 : 3. The date of the whole passage is much disputed, but it clearly goes back to a time when the " El Elyon " of Jerusalem was not fully identified with Yahweh.

(iii) Gen. 24 : 60. The blessing of Rebecca. Metre 3 : 2 (2 : 2). An utterance ensuring the prosperity both of Israel and of Edom. It must come from a time when the traditional hostility between these two peoples had not yet developed.

(iv) Gen. 27 : 27-29. Isaac's blesing of Jacob. Metre uncertain. Jacob is promised political supremacy and material prosperity.

(v) Gen. 27 : 39f. Isaac's curse of Esau. We note the parallel with the preceding ; a play on a Hebrew preposition turns what is a promise of success in the one case into a prediction of adversity in the other. No doubt these two utterances express what every Israelite would have liked to believe as to the fortunes of the two nations concerned.

(vi) Gen. 48 : 15f. Jacob's blessing of Joseph. Metre

3 : 3 (2 : 2 : 2). The language does not suggest an early date.

(vii) Gen. 49 : 2-27. The blessing of Jacob. In form this poem is a spell, that is to say, it purports to be an utterance by the patriarch on his death-bed, which determines the future of the individual tribes. It is, however, much more likely that we have here a collection of little pieces, describing, not the future of each tribe, but its condition at the period of composition. While the passage in its present form appeals to us as a unity, there are not wanting signs to suggest that the individua sections were originally independent, the present arrangement being due to a compiler. Thus, while most of the pieces seem to belong to a comparatively early age—some of them, apparently, come from the age of the Judges— the description of Judah can hardly be placed before the time of David, when the great southern tribe first assumed a position of real leadership in Israel. Reuben still exists, though decline has set in, and Reuben utterly disappeared during the first half of the monarchy. Its territory lay between Gad and Moab, but in the middle of the ninth century B.C. these two had a common frontier. Simeon and Levi (the latter not yet an ecclesiastical body) are, or have recently been, the objects of bitter hatred which may have led to their political overthrow, and we may find a clue in the gruesome story told in Gen. 34. The northern maritime tribes, Zebulun and Asher, still prosper ; the Philistine migration is yet in the future and the Phoenicians do not seem to exercise any authority over their neighbours. Issachar is, apparently, under a foreign yoke, and we remember that the fertile central plains became genuinely Israelite only under David ; they were never included in Saul's dominions, and actually formed the base from which the

Philistines delivered their final attack on him. The description of Dan strongly suggests a location beside a trade route, from which passing caravans could be harassed. Such a situation must have preceded the Danite migration to the north, though the Samson stories may reflect similar conditions. Gad is exposed to *razzias* from the wilderness, a condition which must have been normal through history, and it is equally impossible to guess at a date for the Naphtali verse. Joseph—not yet divided into Ephraim and Manasseh—is at the height of its power and prosperity, and again we should naturally assign this magnificent eulogy to an age preceding that of Saul. Benjamin, too, is yet hardly a royal tribe, and bears the kind of character indicated in the appendix to the Book of Judges. It would be hopeless to look for any uniform metrical arrangement in such a composition, and the final compilation can have taken place only in the first part of the monarchy.

(viii) Num. 6 : 24-26. The Priestly Blessing. Here we have a formula which may be very ancient, though the document in which it is embedded (P) did not reach its present form till after the Exile. But its worth has been recognized through the ages, and it is still used and valued both among Jews and Christians.

(ix) Num. 10 : 35, 36. These verses give the formulae used when the Ark was taken out to battle and when it was restored to its sacred tent. We know that this was done in early days, as is shewn by the narrative in I Sam. 4, but there is no evidence to suggest that the practice was continued under the monarchy. The presumption, therefore, is that these formulae go back to a very early period.

(x)—(xiii). Num. 23 : 7-10, 18-24, 24 : 3-9, 15-19. The Oracles of Balaam. These clearly date from an age which is not later than the ninth century, for there is a strong and confident feeling in them which would have been almost impossible after the appearance of Assyria. All seem to come from the same general source, and, while they may be older than the actual prose narrative in which they are now embedded, they certainly imply a story of Balaam which may have been very nearly identical with that now before us. All four are written in 3 : 3, with hardly any variation, even in our present text, and they attain a high poetic level. It will be noted that the third and fourth open with the same phrases, and this may connect them more closely with one another than with the other two. On the whole the text is better preserved than that of some other ancient poems.

The subject of these utterances is the prosperity of Israel. At the same time the fourth poem contemplates the overthrow of Moab (24 : 17) and, if our text be right, of Edom (24 : 18). There is a distinctly Messianic flavour in the fourth poem, which has led readers to seek, and often to discover, similar doctrines in the other poems, where, however, they are less obvious. Taking the poems all together, the period whose conditions they most clearly suggest is the age of David. This is almost inevitable if we accept 24 : 18 in anything like its present form as an original part of the series, for David was, as far as we know, the first Israelite king to subdue both Moab and Edom, while the " star " and " sceptre " of 24 : 17 would well apply to him in the first instance. The omission or drastic modification of 24 : 18 might allow us to throw the poems as far back as the age of the Judges, for the reference to Moab might be satisfied by Ehud's exploit (Jud. 3), but, on the whole, a rather later date seems more suitable.

(xiv) Num. 24 : 20. Blessing on Amalek. This may be only a fragment of a longer poem. It is ascribed to

Balaam, but is probably a good deal older than the preceding poems. There are two distinct traditions regarding the relations between Amalek and Israel. On the one hand the two are closely allied. Not only is the tribe regarded as an offshoot of Edom (Gen. 36 : 12), of all neighbouring peoples that most nearly related to Israel, but in Jud. 5 : 14 (if our text be right) the tribe of Ephraim is said to be of Amalekite stock. On the other hand there is a strong tradition of inveterate hostility (cf. Ex. 17 : 8-16, Jud. 6, I Sam. 15), traced back to the nomad period, and it was this which prevailed in later Israel. The presumption, then, is that this fragment comes from a comparatively early piece.

(xv) Num. 24 : 21f. Oracle on the Kenites. Here, again, we seem to have a relic of a longer ancient piece. The Kenites seem to have been a nomad tribe of smiths, who wandered from one group to another as their services were needed. We find them among Amalekites in I Sam. 15 : 6, and in the Deborah story (Jud. 4, 5) one of them is as far north as Esdraelon. They were always more or less closely associated with Israel ; according to one form of the tradition it was a Kenite family into which Moses himself married (Jud. 1 : 16), and they united with Judah in their attack on Palestine. When David wished to convince Achish that he had attacked his own people, he described his raids as having been directed against the Negeb of Judah and the Negeb of the Jerachmeelites and the Negeb of the Kenites (I Sam. 27 : 10). Probably they were absorbed in Judah, and this piece can hardly be later than the time of David.

(xvi) Num. 24 : 23f. Oracle on an unknown people. In the present text the Kittim (Cretans), Assyria and the Hebrews are mentioned. But the text is obscure and obviously corrupt ; reasonable sense can be made of this fragment only by conjectural emendation, and we have to admit that we have no longer the clue either to its date or to its original application.

(xvii) Deut. 33. The blessing of Moses. In general form this chapter resembles the blessing of Jacob in Gen. 49, since it contains a series of sections each dealing with a separate tribe. There are, however, certain striking differences between the two. Instead of being a compilation—perhaps even a collection—made of earlier pieces, the blessing of Moses has the appearance of being a single composition, produced by one author. It has an introduction and a conclusion which refer to Israel as a whole, and the metre is nearly consistent 3 : 3 (3 : 3 : 3). The tone of the whole is invariably favourable and sympathetic even where the tribe in question is in difficulties. The poet seems to be aware of some, at least, of the pieces preserved in Gen. 49 ; if the text be correct in both places, Gen. 49 : 26 is directly quoted in Deut. 33 : 16. Each tribe has an introductory title, though the combination of Zebulun and Issachar in vv. 18f suggests that this is a later insertion.

There are also differences in detail. The most obvious is the omission of Simeon, which is to be explained only on the hypothesis that in the writer's time the tribe had already been absorbed in Judah. Reuben, it is true, still exists, but is in a parlous state, and a similar remark may be made of Judah. Levi is now the great ecclesiastical tribe. Benjamin is insignificant but prosperous, while Joseph has attained a unique political status, and is by far the most prominent group in Israel. The division into Ephraim and Manasseh, however, has not yet been recognized. Zebulun and Issachar are closely united, and there is no indication of the latter's subjection. Gad is flourishing ; Dan is already in its northern home.

Naphtali and Asher both enjoy agricultural prosperity, though there is no longer any indication to suggest that the latter now holds the sea-coast.

The poem is thus clearly later than much of the material found in Gen. 49. The most suitable date would be early in the divided monarchy, after the invasion of Sheshonk had spent itself, but before Judah had recovered from the disruption or Damascus had become so powerful as to be a serious menace to Israel. Generally speaking, a date somewhere about 900 B.C. is indicated.

3. *Meshalim*

The term *mashal* is very widely used, and is extremely difficult to define. Comparative philology suggests that the original sense was that of " comparison," and there certainly are *meshalim* which support this derivation. On the other hand the term is applied to a number of pieces which possibly may not be included under this head. The most familiar application is to a short and pithy saying which is intended to sum up human experience in a particular sphere, in other words an epigram or " proverb." Indeed, the Hebrew title of the Book of Proverbs includes a form of the word *meshalim*. But the word is used of many other forms as well. The great taunt-song of Is. 14 : 4-21 is expressly called a *mashal*. So are the utterances of Balaam ; the word may once have been used to describe a spell. A *mashal*, especially in early times, was not necessarily poetical at all. The popular phrase—" Is Saul also among the prophets ? " is called a *mashal* in I Sam. 10 : 12, though not in I Sam. 19 : 24. The group is very difficult to define, and possibly some of the pieces here included in it should be classed under other heads.

(i) Gen. 25 : 23. The Oracle of Rebecca. Here the

future relations of her twin sons are described ; if their
names had been mentioned the verse would clearly have
been a "spell." Probably, like most such sayings, it
represents history (from the Israelite point of view)
rather than prediction.

(ii) Num. 12 : 6-8. Moses and the Prophets. Here
we have a real comparison between two classes, the one
consisting of Moses only, the other including all normal
prophets.

(iii) Josh. 10 : 12. The Sun at Gibeon. The interpretation of Joshua's prayer has been widely discussed.
The following verse, coming probably from a date later
than Joshua, assumes that it was a request for the
miraculous prolongation of the day, and so the ancient
Book of Yashar understood it (v. 13). Other suggestions
are that the daylight seemed to be lengthened as the
pursuing Israelites crossed the last main ridge on their
way down to the plain, and that the western light was
still strong, or that the words imply the cessation of
bright sunshine which was blinding the Israelites, through
the coming up of a thunderstorm. It is clear that the
saying is very ancient.

(iv) Jud. 9 : 8-15. Jotham's Fable. It may be questioned whether this should really be classed as poetry.
In spite of the general similarity of the sentences, they
vary a good deal in metrical form, and there is hardly a
trace of genuine parallelism. It may, however, be
claimed that the modelling of successive verses in the same
way may be regarded as a kind of parallelism, and on
this ground the passage might be included among the early
poems of Israel. It is certainly a "parable," and on this
ground may be described as a *mashal*, though the term is
not applied to it. But whatever its form or class, it gives
us a good example of imaginative and rhetorical speech.

(v) Jud. 14 : 14, 18a. Samson's riddle and the answer. Both these short single-line sentences may be regarded as typical *meshalim*.

(vi) Jud. 14 : 18b. Samson's rejoinder. A saying of exactly the same type as the last.

(vii) Jud. 15 : 16. Samson on one of his Victories. This is a typical 2 : 2 couplet. The phrase " heaps upon heaps " does not bring out the Hebrew paronomasia ; the words used closely resemble the original for " ass," and the second should probably be rendered as a verb.

(viii) I Sam. 15 : 22f. Samuel's condemnation of Saul. V. 22 is a characteristic 4 : 3 ; v. 23 probably 3 : 3, an arrangement which suggests that two utterances, originally distinct, have been combined. Certainly v. 22 throws back into a comparatively early period a doctrine which is not prominent until the eighth century, and the incident recorded in I Sam. 13 : 8-14 hardly indicates that Samuel put a comparatively low value on sacrifice and its correct forms.

(ix) I Sam. 15 : 33. The doom of Agag. Another typical *mashal*, in 2 : 2 rhythm.

(x) I Sam. 18 : 7 (also 21 : 12 and 29 : 5). The Women's Song over David and Saul ; rhythm 3 : 2. This must have been a very familiar saying, and is just the sort of sentence which the dancing women would repeat over and over again. In the East the constant reiteration of a short phrase is a characteristic form of expression, either giving vent to emotion or exciting the singers and hearers to a high pitch. A good modern example is to be found in the Indian *bhajan*.

(xi) I Sam. 24 : 13. David to Saul ; rhythm probably 3 : 3. The term *mashal* is expressly used here, and the words may be a formula of exculpation.

(xii) II Sam. 12 : 1-4. Nathan's Parable. As with

Jotham's parable, we have here a piece which, in spite of its high value, we should probably not class as poetry at all. It is a straight-forward narrative, rendered extremely impressive, not only by the circumstances, but also by the form, in which the two men are so strongly contrasted.

(xiii) II Sam. 20 : 1. A Slogan of Revolt. Placed in the mouth of one Sheba, this saying clearly represents a feeling current throughout northern Israel during the reigns of David and Solomon.

(xiv) I Kgs. 12 : 16. Another, and slightly different form of the preceding. The variations rather tend to shew the popularity of the saying, and illustrate the fact that the union of north and south was always rather artificial. It was not, in fact, till after the fall of Samaria in 721 B.C. that the hopes of all Israel centred in the House of David.

4. Paeans

Poems of this type form a well-marked class, and are easy to identify. They are always introduced with reference to some historical event, though it is possible that sometimes the hymn of thanksgiving and triumph is a later composition, applied by a poet of another age to some glorious happening in the past. It is worth noting that in Israel these songs of victory were never merely an expression of the conqueror's pride or a vindictive gloating over a fallen enemy. With one consent the authors ascribe the success to Yahweh, and give to him their thanks and praise.

(i) Ex. 15 : 1-18. The Song of Moses at the Red Sea. This is a magnificent hymn of triumph, celebrating the exploits of Yahweh in bringing his people across the Red Sea and planting them in Palestine. The prevailing metre is 2 : 2, with five 3 : 2 lines ; three " irregular lines " may owe their present form to slight textual corruption. While the structure is not uniformly strophic, the poem is readily divisible into three well-marked sections. At the beginning of each the poet breaks into rapture of praise, and then describes the particular event which has called for his enthusiasm at the moment. Thus vv. 1-2 introduce the first of Yahweh's mighty deeds, the destruction of Pharaoh's army in the Red Sea. In v. 6, again, the writer breaks out into praise, and then gives a second account of the crossing. A third burst of laudation in v. 11 leads up to the passage through Moab and Edom and the establishment of Israel with its sanctuary in Canaan, while the poem closes with the ascription of eternal sovereignty to Yahweh. Each of these three sections is in a sense self-contained, but that does not prevent the poem from giving the general appearance of being a unity.

Clearly the hymn comes from a later time than that of Moses. The opening verse, it is true, is practically identical with the song of Miriam given in v. 21, and may have been used as a theme which this poet sought to expand. But, in addition to the historical references to the last stages of the wanderings (vv. 14-16), the anachronism of introducing the Philistines before the Israelite conquest (v. 14), the settlement and the establishment of a sanctuary (v. 17), there are other signs which make a very early date highly improbable. The description of the sea standing up like walls in v. 8 recalls the later of the two accounts of the crossing interwoven in Ex. 14. This does not, of course, necessarily mean that the poem is to be relegated to an age later than P, for that form of the tradition may be much older than its embodiment in the priestly record, but it does demand time for the growth of the highly miraculous element which is absent from the earlier strand in Ex. 14. Further, the language has certain characteristic marks of the later style, and, all things considered, it is difficult to assign this hymn to an age earlier than the middle period of the monarchy.

(ii) Ex. 15 : 21. The Song of Miriam. This consists of a 2 : 2 couplet, which appears in a slightly modified form at the head of the last piece. As suggested above, it may well have been the ancient celebration of the event to which it is ascribed, and have served a later poet as a subject which he has expanded.

(iii) Jud. 5. The Song of Deborah. Here we have one of the great triumphal odes of literature. By common consent it goes back to the period of the events which it describes, and was almost certainly the work of an eye-witness. It is true that, in all probability, Deborah herself was not the author, for she is directly addressed in v. 12, and the latter part of v. 7 is most probably couched in the second person, not the first—" till thou, Deborah, didst arise, thou didst arise, a mother in Israel." But the exact authorship is of little moment in such a case as this, and it is generally admitted that we have here the most ancient poetic composition of any length which has come down to us from Israel. The metre is uncertain, perhaps owing to the rather extensive textual corruption to which the Song has been subject through the centuries, but the original basis seems to have been 2 : 2.

As a work of art the Song of Deborah stands very high. Its vigour, freshness, wealth of imagination, and vividness, make it a stirring and powerful poem. It gives us a unique picture of the conditions of life in Israel during the period between the conquest and the establishment of the monarchy. We see the new-comers divided among themselves and still clinging to their tribal organization. They have not yet advanced far in civilization, and their enemies are far better trained and armed. There is no central authority, except in so far as an individual may arise from time to time and bring the tribes together with an appeal issued in the name of Yahweh. It is noticeable that when any member of the whole fails to respond or to do its part, the offender is condemned for not coming to the help of Yahweh, not for failing Israel. Further, we note that in certain circumstances the wild dash of the Israelite hordes more than compensates for their inferior equipment and discipline. We realize that it was these two features, the unifying power of their religion and their inspired battle-fury, which gave the Israelites their dominant position in Palestine.

(iv) I Sam. 2 : 1-10. The Song of Hannah. Here, again, we have a great ode of triumph. The metre is uniformly 3 : 3 (3 : 3 : 3). The piece can hardly have been composed for the circumstances to which it is applied, for, except for a single reference in v. 5, there is nothing peculiarly suitable to Hannah's position. Even in v. 5 the suggestion that the mother of many children languishes is hardly borne out by the narrative, and there can be little doubt that the hymn commemorates some military victory, and that the mention of the childless mother is simply figurative. The date is quite uncertain. As it stands, the hymn might come from the monarchy, but v. 6 is held by some to indicate a belief in the resurrection. If this interpretation is correct, then we must assume the piece to be post-exilic, and the reference to a king in v. 10 must be taken in a purely messianic sense. In any case it is generally agreed that the song was no part of the original book, and should be regarded as a later insertion.

5. *Dirges*

The dirge was a common form of poetry in ancient Israel. It seems to have been normally produced at funerals, and there was a special profession of trained wailing women (cf. Jer. 9 : 17-22). We gather that there was a magical element in their work, demanding an esoteric knowledge handed down from teacher to pupil, and occasionally receiving additions which were in accord with the general trend. It seems probable that the custom of pronouncing dirges over the dead was a relic of days when men believed that the spirit might return and injure or at least annoy the living. It was, therefore, imperative that measures should be taken which would keep the dead in their place, either by weaving about them an insurmountable spell or by making them so satisfied with their new lot that they would be unwilling to leave it. A further motive may well have been the desire to propitiate the dead and ensure their good will, so that even if they did reappear in spirit, they would do good and not harm to the survivors. A dirge, then, is often a panegyric, and necessarily took this form where the original aim was forgotten, and it became the outpouring of a loving and grief-stricken heart. The two dirges which have survived in the historical books of the Old Testament are of this type. Both are ascribed to David, and his authorship has never seriously been doubted.

(i) II Sam. 1 : 19-27. Saul and Jonathan. This is one of the loveliest poems of sorrow in literature. The metre is that most frequently used in dirges, 3 : 2, with a fairly large proportion in this case of 2 : 2. The text is, apparently, not well preserved, but in a number of places it can be corrected by the LXX. We know nothing of David which presents him in a better light. We can understand his references to Jonathan, who was always his friend, but the poet speaks with almost equal affection of Saul. All the mistrust, treachery and persecution are now forgotten, and death has allowed only the king's virtues and beneficent acts to survive.

(ii) II Sam. 3 : 33f. Abner. As compared with the preceding this is very short and lacks intensity of feeling. We can hardly avoid the impression that we have here only a fragment, especially when we note that the second part of v. 34 is difficult to fit into any regular metrical scheme, while the remainder is in 3 : 2.

6. *Psalms*

In addition to the poems mentioned, we have from time to time Psalms preserved in books other than the Psalter. A number may be found in the prophetic books ; Jonah, Nahum and Habakkuk, for example, contain one each, and several appear in Isaiah and Jeremiah. In the prose books we have instances where pieces now included in the Psalter are quoted at length ; e.g., II Sam. 22 is identical with Ps. 18, and I Chron. 16 : 8-36 is composed of Ps. 105 : 1-15, Ps. 96 and Ps. 106 : 1, 47f. There are, however, two which do not appear elsewhere, and one which is also recorded in the Book of Isaiah. These are :

(i) Deut. 32 : 1-43. The Song of Moses. In form this poem, like Pss. 78, 105, 106, is a historical record of the behaviour of Israel during the nomad period, contrasting the two main *motifs*, the infidelity of Israel and the loving constancy of Yahweh. It has been described as a compendium of the prophetic teaching, and certainly sums up the story of Israel's relations with her God. It is rich in language and spiritual vigour ; some of its phrases have become classical sayings. It clearly comes from a much later age than that of Moses, for the events

c

to which it alludes have taken place in the distant past (v. 7). It may be assigned with some confidence to the latter half of the Judahite monarchy, though opinions differ as to whether it came from the eighth or from the seventh century.

(ii) II Sam. 23 : 1-7. The Last Words of David. As in Ps. 1 and elsewhere, a contrast is drawn between the fate of the righteous and that of the wicked. Though the piece is put into the mouth of David, there is a general feeling that it comes from a later time, and is out of place in its present context. The text is obscure, and may be corrupt in places.

(iii) II Kgs. 19 : 21-28 (see also Is. 37 : 22-29). An oracle of Isaiah. Strictly speaking, this passage is a purely prophetic utterance, taken by the compiler of Kings from a collection of material relating to Isaiah. It is, indeed, probable that it was not originally included in the narratives which the compiler used, but was added at a later date by an editor who sought thus to complete the narrative of Isaiah. It forms a taunt-song, of less vigour and power than that preserved in Is. 14, but still of considerable literary and religious value. In the true spirit of Isaiah it predicts the coming overthrow of Assyria, who has defied, not Israel, but Yahweh himself. There are, however, phrases which suggest Deutero-Isaiah rather than the eighth century prophet.

IV

JOB : I

It will be almost universally agreed that in the Book of Job we have the supreme literary masterpiece of the Hebrew genius. Indeed, it is not impossible to claim that, taking into consideration all those factors which go to make up a great work of art, it will be found second to none in all the range of human writing. There can be no real greatness in literature apart from an intense passion for truth and that courage which such passion carries with it. A style which is at once lofty, dignified, and rich in word and thought is a *sine qua non*. We inevitably demand not only some appreciation of nature, but also deep insight into the character of personality, human and divine. There must, too, be humour, by which we mean no superficial attempt to be " funny," but a deep sense of incongruity between things as they ought to be, things as they are said to be, and things as they are. Such true humour may be grim indeed, but it is genuine. Finally, all these qualities will be wasted unless they are used to treat a theme of importance, weight, and even grandeur.

There are certain productions of man's spirit which exhibit several or even all of these things in a superlative degree. In English we have Milton, the poet who, in some ways, approaches nearest to the author of Job— but who would charge Milton with humour? The scene in *Paradise Lost* Bk. VI, where the Satanic host invents artillery (of the seventeenth century type !)

would alone suffice to prove the poet's deficiency in this respect. Shakespeare, though at times reaching the confines of the sublime theme, was necessarily limited by the conventions of a secularized theatre. Lucretius, who in so many ways reminds us of Job, lacks the intensity of personal feeling which gives so much of his force to the Hebrew poet. The three who, perhaps, approach most nearly to the Biblical author are Aeschylus, Dante, and Goethe (in *Faust*), and none of them quite rises to the height of Job.

The subject of this poem is the most serious problem that has ever troubled the human mind. How can the hypothesis of a perfectly good ruler of the Universe be reconciled with facts relating to pain? It is not so much the existence of pain that raises the question; that may find a comparatively simple answer. But how are we to defend its distribution? There is so much which seems to be causeless and purposeless. This problem is faced with a stark passion for truth, which allows the poet to shrink from no conclusion which the facts may present to him, and to take refuge in no half-hearted, superficial, or conventional explanation. He has a profound sense of the gulf which separates accepted views and statements from the actual truth, and seldom, if ever, has a great poet ventured on so ruthless an exposure of the futility inherent in beliefs which rest on too shallow foundations. The author of Job, too, has a power of reading the depths of the human heart which has never been surpassed and seldom equalled. He sees below the surface of personality, and with surety identifies those hidden motives of which men are themselves so often unconscious. Finally all this is expressed in language which deserves to stand in the very front rank. Here, no doubt, the author has the advantage of writing in

Hebrew, one of the most musical and stately of all the varied tongues spoken by man. The immense strength of its accent gives it a rhythmic movement which we miss in languages which have a slighter stress. The paucity of adjectives adds to the dignity and impressiveness of the style, and the absence of a large stock of abstract terms leads the poet to use imagery and metaphor in its place. Not a few of these are drawn from the world of nature, where the writer was a keen observer, though, not unnaturally, he sometimes fell into the errors common to his age.

What has just been said, however, refers only to the main poem included in the Book of Job, and this leads us to a consideration of its actual form. As it stands, it falls obviously into three sections. The first, occupying chs. 1-2, is a prose narrative describing the state and misfortunes of the hero. Then follows a large section in verse, ending with 42 : 6, containing for the most part a dialogue between Job and his friends. Finally there is a short section in prose, 42 : 7-17, which gives some account of Job's restoration to health and of his later period of prosperity.

The question naturally arises : Are we to regard the whole as the work of a single author ? Did he write the narrative of events and then throw his meditations on them into poetic form ? Such a method would have been unusual, but we do not know enough of ancient literature, and, in particular, of Hebrew literature, to say that this view is impossible. It is, nevertheless, open to us to believe that the poet found an older narrative and that he used it as a framework into which he fitted his own poem. It is, of course, clear that the various parts are not independent of one another. The poetic section assumes throughout the story told in the first two chapters, though occasionally the poet appears to overlook details, e.g., in 14 : 21 and 19 : 17, Job speaks as if his children were still living. And the last section is obviously intended to give a happy ending to the story, though not necessarily to the poem.

Now there is no doubt that Job was a familiar figure in Hebrew literary tradition. There is a reference to him in Ez. 14 : 14, 20, where he is mentioned along with Noah and Daniel in terms which suggest that he was a man so conspicuous for his righteousness that his very presence in a sinful community might be expected to ward off its punishment—a hope which was not to be fulfilled. The character thus ascribed to him is quite in harmony with the picture presented by both prose sections in the Book of Job, though it does not necessarily follow that these, in their present form, were known to Ezekiel, still less that the prophet was acquainted with the whole book. There was a well-known story current in ancient Mesopotamia, telling of a righteous king who was subjected to great misfortune, and some students have connected this with the narratives of Job. The differences, however, are so great as to preclude any theory of a common literary origin, though the type of story may well have been handed down with numerous local modifications from very ancient times. At the same time, there is nothing in the first two chapters of the book which deters us from believing that this tale, at any rate, was in existence before the time of Ezekiel. The conclusion, too, may be taken as having formed a part of the same original narrative as the introduction. Stress has sometimes been laid on minor discrepancies (e.g., in the epilogue there is no mention of the Satan, who is the cause of all the trouble in the prologue), but there is no serious divergence between the two prose sections, either in style or in subject matter. The love of a happy ending was so strong in the ancient mind that it is difficult to imagine a story starting as ch. 1f, and not ending as the book actually does end.

While, however, we may fairly regard the prose sections of the book as being parts of a single whole, dating back to the pre-exilic period, it by no means follows that the book as it now stands is a unity. Between the prose and the poem there are variations and even discrepancies which have led many to believe that they are the work, not merely of different authors, but of different literary periods. It has often been observed that there is a marked difference in the use of the divine names. The prose narrative places Job in the land of Uz, i.e., it probably regards him as an Edomite. Yet the name of the special God of Israel, Yahweh, is frequently used, even by Job himself; the more general term Elohim is also common. The former is found only six times in the whole length of the poetic section, and of those six occurrences only one is in the dialogue itself. Elohim, too, appears six times in the verse portions of the book, four of these being in the dialogue proper. Three divine names are characteristic of the poem. One is El, a term common elsewhere, which appears between fifty and sixty times and is even more general than Elohim. Shaddai is used some thirty times in this book and about twenty in various other parts of the Hebrew Bible. Most striking is the term Eloah, apparently a singular formed artificially from the common plural Elohim. Out of about fifty-five occurrences of this form, no less than forty are in the Book of Job. None of these three is used in our present text of the prose sections.

It is difficult to find a valid reason why an author should thus vary the use of the divine names. We can understand that he might wish to place his discussion on a wider base than that offered by Israel alone, and therefore chose an Edomite and put general language into his mouth. But would not these considerations equally operate in the prose portions? In particular, why should the narrator have put the name Yahweh into Job's mouth in one of the very few places where the hero's words are actually quoted (1 : 21)? Here we certainly have a discrepancy, though it does not amount to a contradiction, and may be due to some cause which we are unable to conjecture.

There appears to be some slight difference in the treatment of the disease from which Job suffers. In 2 : 7 it is described as a " boil," a general term which is used in Lev. 13 in connection with the symptoms of leprosy, though it is not strictly applied to the disease itself. Such references as we have in the poem make it clear that the author regarded Job as a leper, suffering from an advanced form of the complaint. It is something incurable, but comparatively slow, though it will certainly grant the sufferer only a few more years of life (16 : 22). His body is covered with horrible sores, forming crusts which break and run, serving as a home for loathsome parasites (7 : 5), while the patient is afflicted with terrifying nightmares, from which he awakes to find himself choking— due to similar sores in the throat (7 : 14f). It is difficult to see why the prose narrator should not have used one of the terms for leprosy if he had identified the disease as certainly as the poet has done.

Differences in the point of view are even more striking. We cannot lay any stress on the fact that the Satan is not mentioned in the poem, though it is on his initiative that Job's sorrows have befallen him. The scene in heaven is naturally unknown to the earthly characters, and even in other parts of the prose narrative neither Job nor any one else is aware of the real cause of his troubles. But it is worthy of note that the whole conception of piety seems to be fundamentally different. The prose narrative makes Job meek and submissive to the divine will, accepting with resignation and patience whatever lot it may please the supreme Wisdom to assign him. In the poem, this is very much the view taken by the friends ; it is emphatically not the attitude of Job himself, and no small part of the dialogue (on Job's side) is an energetic refusal to accept the position which the others try to force on him. Here we have something which is not merely a discrepancy ; it is a real contradiction, and many students find it impossible to resolve it on the hypothesis of unity in authorship.

Doubtless other points may be urged, but to a sympathetic reader there is one which probably outweighs all the rest. This is the totally different tone of the two sections. The introduction and conclusion, though not without feeling for the sufferer, are yet written from the outside. The narrator is describing what he (or some other) has seen but not felt in his own case. The poet, on the other hand, writes with his own heart's blood. He is himself the hero, he has suffered, perhaps not as Job suffered in every detail, but he is certainly a leper. The spiritual history, too, is that of the author himself. No mere outsider could have given us the intensity and passion with which the great battle of the soul is depicted, the gloom and despair, the alternations between the faint gleams of hope and the black reality which extinguishes them, the spirit of courageous revolt which does not shrink from the apparent blasphemy of Job's appeal from the God of popular theology to God as He really must be, the supreme leap of faith by which the sufferer does at

c*

last plant his foot upon solid ground, and, finally, the contented submission in which he reposes when he has seen God face to face. These things have come from the poet's own soul ; they are not the experiences of another in which he has had no direct share.

We may, then, attempt to reconstruct the general history of the book in its simplest form. There existed a popular story which told of a righteous man who, nevertheless, suffered unparalleled disasters. These were due, not to any sin which he had committed, but to the demands made by an official of the divine court. This person's title was " the Satan," a word which originally meant simply " adversary." His function was to test men, and to see whether their outward appearance of goodness was an index of their true character. Challenged by Yahweh in the heavenly council, the Satan expressed his doubts as to the depth and genuineness of Job's religion, and was allowed to put the man to the severest test. First Job lost his property and his children ; he still remained firm, and at a second council the Satan was given permission to attack him personally. He struck Job with terrible boils and reduced him to the lowest condition. Even so, he continued steadfast in his patient submission to the will of God, and not even the despairing advice of his wife could shake him. Three friends came to comfort him. Their conversation is lost, but it seems that the friends blamed Yahweh for Job's calamities. It must be remembered that all the earthly characters are ignorant of the heavenly councils and of the real cause of Job's troubles. Job, on the other hand, maintained his correct attitude, and at length Yahweh himself appeared, condemned the friends, justified Job, and, ultimately, restored to him greater prosperity than he had previously known.

This story took written form at some time during the second half of the monarchy. A later poet, who had himself suffered much as Job had done, if not more terribly, took the story as a basis for his own meditations, cut out the existing dialogue between Job and the friends, and inserted an account of his own spiritual struggles, retaining only the beginning and the end of the story.

We now turn to the poetical centre of the book. It falls into three distinct parts, the first, containing chs. 3–31 is a dialogue between Job and the three friends who were mentioned in the popular story. Then follows, in chs. 32–37, a speech, or rather a series of speeches, from a new character named Elihu. In 38 : 1 Yahweh appears in a storm-cloud (probably a detail derived from the popular tale) and speaks in such fashion that Job falls prostrate in utter submission (38 : 1-42 : 6). The first section is much the longest, and is symmetrically arranged. Job speaks first, and answers each of his friends, who speak in turn, so that the order is Job, Eliphaz, Job, Bildad, Job, Zophar, Job, Eliphaz, etc. There are three " rounds " to the debate, but in the third round, according to our present text Bildad has only a few verses, while Zophar does not speak at all. Elihu has four speeches with no intervention by Job ; the second and third are introduced with the words, " And Elihu answered and said," which do not, however, necessarily imply that another person has just spoken. In the third poetic section, chs. 38–39 are occupied by a speech of Yahweh. There is, apparently, no answer from Job, and in 40 : 1f, Yahweh challenges him. To this Job replies briefly in 40 : 3-5, and Yahweh delivers another speech, which continues to the end of ch. 41. In 42 : 1-6 Job makes his final submission.

Grave doubts have arisen as to whether the whole of

this poetic section is original. In particular, the speeches of Elihu have roused suspicion. It is clear that there was no such person in the old popular story, or we should have heard his name at the end of ch. 2. He is introduced abruptly, after every other character has spoken, and though this is explained by the statement that he is younger than any of the rest, we can hardly avoid the feeling that his presence may be due to a later poet than the author of the preceding dialogue. It is strange, again, to find that, whereas Job has had something to say in reply to every utterance of the other three, he is completely silent in the presence of Elihu. It is true that Elihu rebukes him, and this might have led Job to be still from a sense of shame, but the sufferer has received yet harsher treatment from the others, and has certainly not refrained from reply. This absence of remark from Job is the more striking when we observe that the Elihu section is broken up into several speeches, and Job might with propriety have intervened at the end of each. Further, Job's last utterances in chs. 29-31 have involved a passionate appeal to Yahweh to appear and meet his challenge. The response comes in 38 : 1, and Elihu certainly interrupts the natural course of events. Nor do the Elihu speeches themselves seem to justify the delay. Their style is lofty and sustained, having many of the qualities of the best Hebrew poetry, but an acute critic may well find that they do not reach quite the same level as the earlier parts of the book. They add little to the actual debate ; Elihu follows the other friends in believing that Job's sufferings are punitive, and in suggesting complete submission as the only course for Job to pursue. He does, it is true, state explicitly that Job's real sin is self-righteousness, which would not have been discovered but for his sufferings, but this is implied in a great deal of what the friends have already said. Finally we note the strongly contrasted attitude of the writer here and in the earlier section. As we have already noted, in the main dialogue it is Job who is the hero ; we may go even further and say that Job is the author himself, at least in feeling and in thought. The composer of the Elihu speeches, on the other hand, is certainly looking at Job from an external standpoint, and fails to enter into his experiences even so far as Eliphaz does in his opening words. We cannot avoid the conviction that, to put the case in its simplest form, the author of chs. 3–31 is sympathetic to Job ; the author of 32–37 is critical or even hostile.

The Elihu speeches, then, do not fit easily into the general scheme of the book, they add little of value to its subject, and they present us with a general point of view quite different from that of the main dialogue. It is, then, natural to suppose that they are a later insertion. This will be widely acknowledged, and the only way in which the unity of authorship can be plausibly maintained is to suggest that the original author, in his later years, realized the imperfections of his attitude, and tried to remedy his mistake by stating the truth as he now saw it. This is the view actually held by more than one prominent scholar, though it involves certain difficulties. If, as seems almost certain, the poet were a leper, and his disease were far advanced at the time when the poem was written, it is hardly likely that he would have lived so long as the theory requires. Even if he had felt that his earlier position was wrong, his simplest method of correction would have been to destroy his original production. These difficulties, however, are not final, and the hypothesis of a revision by the same author cannot be excluded, even though we may feel that it is less probable than the view that the two sections come from quite different hands.

There are shorter sections which have roused the suspicion of many readers. Most conspicuous among these is the poem on Wisdom in ch. 28. It is a very fine piece of writing, and holds an important place in the development of Hebrew religious and philosophical thinking. But it interrupts the dialogue at a point where the tension is very high, and not merely has no bearing on its immediate context, but deals with a theme and reflects an attitude quite alien to those of the book as a whole. We can hardly doubt that here, too, we have a passage which has been inserted at a comparatively late period into the text.

There are two passages in the divine speeches towards the end of the book which are also regarded as being possible interpolations. These are the descriptions of the hippopotamus and of the crocodile in 40 : 15-41 : 34. Others of God's creatures are mentioned in these chapters, it is true, but these two passages are much longer and more artificial than the rest. They contain an unusual number of rare words, or even of words not found elsewhere in this or in any other book of the Bible. And to some readers they interrupt the progress of the poem, which has begun an actual conversation between Yahweh and Job in 40 : 1-14, continued in 42 : 1. But here the question of originality cannot be finally settled, since the answer must depend to a large extent on the literary taste and feeling of the individual reader.

Before leaving the external study of the book, there is one other point which demands attention. It has already been remarked that in the third round of the debate Bildad speaks very briefly and Zophar is silent altogether. This might be explained as indicating that the friends were conscious of having been worsted in the discussion, to such an extent that one of them had little to say, and another could find no answer at all to Job. But the character of the friends (and particularly of these two) as depicted in their earlier speeches does not harmonize with this view. Bildad has always had a good deal to say, especially since he has given up direct argument and fallen back on sheer abuse of Job. Zophar is even less likely to have been silenced by lack of grounds on which Job's position can be logically disputed, for he is uniformly pictured as dogmatic, aggressive, and somewhat conceited. It seems hardly likely that a poet with the power of such delicate character-drawing as is shewn in this book would have allowed his characters so complete a change in disposition. But when we come to look closely into chs. 25–27, several surprising facts emerge. Two passages are assigned to Job which are utterly unlike his usual utterances. These are chs. 26, and 27 : 7-23. Both are in the style and adopt the point of view characteristic of the friends, and if our present text is right in assigning them to Job, we have to assume sarcasm of a type which he does not exhibit elsewhere. If, on the other hand, we may assume that at this point the text has got into some disorder, and that a section has been altogether lost, the position becomes natural. It is generally held that the introductory verse in 26 : 1, which ascribes the following passage to Job, is an error, and that 26 : 2-4 originally formed the opening of Bildad's third speech, while the remainder of ch. 26 also belongs to it. Now 27 : 2-6, 11, 12, are quite suitable to Job, and fall in with the rest of what he has consistently said throughout the poem, but the remainder of ch. 27, again, is exactly in line with the attitude of the friends. It is, then, widely held that a section has been lost, including the end of

Job's reply to Bildad and the opening of Zophar's third
speech. The original order, then, may well have been
as follows :—

25 : 1 ⎫
26 : 2-4 ⎪
25 : 2-6 ⎬ Bildad's third speech.
26 : 5-14 ⎭

26 : 1 ⎫
27 : 2-6, 11, 12 ⎬ Part of Job's reply to Bildad.

27 : 7, 10, 13-23 Part of Zophar's third speech.

The natural continuation with Job's speech in chs.
29–31 then follows.

Like many other ancient Hebrew books, then, the
Book of Job seems to have had a history, in the course
of which it underwent modifications and additions.
Besides the sections already discussed, we have reason to
suspect a number of other insertions. The great majority
of the latter are very short, and most of them consist only
of a few words each. The original text of the LXX,
which was a good deal shorter than our present Hebrew
text, enables us to detect a large number of these. There
may be instances in which the Egyptian tradition
shortened an existing sentence, but as a rule the internal
evidence justifies the Greek of this book as against
the Massoretic text, at least so far as the length of verses is
concerned. But we cannot regret these additions and
alterations, for, even if they do not help us to the message
of the actual author, they testify to the fact that the book
was known and used, and they give us much light on the
way in which men's thought about God moved during the
centuries.

It remains to consider the date of the main poem.
Here we have one interesting piece of direct evidence.
In Job 7 : 17f we have a bitter parody of phrases found in

Ps. 8 : 4. The book is, therefore, later than Ps. 8.
But when was Ps. 8 written? All we know is that it
may not be put late in the post-exilic period. For other
evidence as to the date of Job we have to rely on what we
find in the text itself. This certainly points to a post-
exilic age. There are, from time to time, Aramaic forms
and constructions which we do not find in pre-exilic
Hebrew. The main theme of the poem implies an
advanced form of prophetic teaching, involving not
merely the intensely ethical character of Yahweh as
stated by the pre-exilic prophets, but also a pure monotheism of a kind which first developed during the exile.
This has now become so well established that there is no
longer any need to emphasize it ; the writer assumes a
monotheistic order in the universe, and it never occurs
to him to insist on it. There may be references to astral
cults in 31 : 26-28 and elsewhere, but they obviously
play only a small part in the life of the writer and his
contemporaries. There is no established doctrine of a
life after death ; indeed the book contains one of the
earliest efforts to reach this truth. We may, then, be
sure that it is to be placed in the post-exilic age, well
after the restoration of the Jewish community to its own
land, but at the same time, it must not be too late. A
date at the end of the fifth century or the beginning of the
fourth would satisfy all the conditions indicated in the
book itself. Nearer it is impossible to go. But the exact
date is a matter of very slight importance. Beyond what
his poem tells us, we know nothing of the author—not
even his name. But he has given us a work which is
timeless, handling a question to which man may never find
a complete answer ; the value and direct application of
the book will endure as long as man seeks to understand
the mysteries of God.

The question with which the book deals is the age-long problem of suffering. We should look with some care at the terms we are using. To the adherents of most religions suffering is a fact, and a terrible fact, but it is not a *problem*. We can use that word only when we are confronted with a fact which appears to contradict our faith. Faith, in one important aspect of that complex idea, is the adoption of a hypothesis as a working basis for life, and it is inevitable, in view of our human limitations, that from time to time we should realize that there may be, indeed there are, points at which our hypothesis is either inaccurate or incomplete. Rightly treated, a discordant fact should enable us to amend our hypothesis—possibly even to discard it altogether. But neither the man of science nor the man of religion will lightly throw over what he and his predecessors have won with long research and thought. Adams did not reject the theory of gravitation because the movements of the planet Uranus did not correspond exactly to the course which that doctrine prescribed ; he used the new and discordant facts as a basis for further calculation, and, in the discovery of Neptune triumphantly vindicated the original theory, and added to man's knowledge of the solar system. So in progressive religion, men will not readily abandon a well-grounded hypothesis ; they will rather meditate and seek until the obtrusive fact is fitted into the scheme and leads to fuller knowledge.

Now suffering is a problem only when it confronts the hypothesis that the whole universe of nature and of man is governed and controlled by a perfectly good, omnipotent Person. Otherwise it is easy to explain either on the basis of mere chance or on that of conflicting superior wills, some of which are not good. It is even possible to assume that the governing power is evil, but that at once raises the problem of the large amount of good which exists in the world. For the thorough-going pessimist the problem of good is even more serious than the problem of evil is for the optimist.

Much of the suffering in human life is easily understood on an optimistic basis. It is a necessary corollary of free will, and may be directive, punitive, purifying, or educational. But there remain cases in which none of these explanations will apply, and there are countless others in which the degree of suffering seems out of all proportion to the cause or the effect. The great question is raised more by the distribution of suffering than by its existence.

There are two points which stand out as we enter the discussion of the matter. One is that the *problem* of suffering could have arisen in the ancient world only on the basis of such teaching as that which the great prophets of Israel gave. To them Yahweh was supreme over men and over all other gods. He was also perfectly righteous and loving. Each sin must be punished ; every good deed rewarded. Yet this poetic distribution of justice is very far from being the experience of the world. How can the facts be reconciled with the theory ? In the second place, given the work of men like Isaiah, Amos and Hosea, the problem was bound to arise. Men are slow to realize the implications and bearing of their own beliefs, but, sooner or later, the human mind will awake to the incongruity between theory and fact, and will try to resolve it. It is to Habakkuk, as far as we know, that we owe the first statement of the problem of suffering—" Too pure of eyes art thou, to look upon evil, and to gaze on iniquity thou art not able. Why then dost thou gaze on the treacherous, art silent when the wicked swalloweth up the man that is more righteous than he " (Hab. 1 : 13).

Jeremiah, too, was faced with the same difficulty through his own experience (Jer. 12 : 1-3). He found no answer at all, but was compelled to turn to his own practical difficulties. Habakkuk won the conviction that " the righteous shall live by his fidelity " (2 : 4)—a phrase whose meaning is still a matter of dispute, but which seems to teach that patient endurance will win its reward in the end. Other solutions were offered by later thinkers in Israel. Men like the author of Ps. 37 roundly asserted —in defiance of fact—that the wicked were sure to meet with disaster in the long run, and the righteous would certainly be suitably rewarded—the successful swindler will ultimately perish in destitution while the honest pauper will die a millionaire. A real contribution was made by the writer of Isaiah 53, who came to the conclusion that suffering had a vicarious efficiency, and that the happiness of some might be won by the misery of others. The perfectly surrendered servant of God would gladly accept all the pain if he but knew that others would profit by it. To the author of Ps. 49 both the adversity of the good and the prosperity of the bad were illusory, since both terminated with death. The mystic to whom we owe Ps. 73 found peace in the knowledge of God's eternal friendship, and in fellowship with Him experienced a joy which death itself could neither interrupt nor destroy. Christian doctrine goes further still, and in the Cross of Christ offers a profound alleviation, if not a solution. Suffering is not merely a human experience, it is also divine, and therefore there must be a solution, even though it be beyond the grasp of the finite intellect.

It is in the Book of Job that we meet with the most thorough and complete attempt to answer the great question. We have to remember that, at the outset, the discussion is based on the belief that death was the end of all relations between man and God. True, some kind of personal identity was retained in Sheol, but God was not there ; the whole drama of the religious life, the relations between man and God, must be played out on the stage of this life. With this background we can proceed to a more detailed study of the book itself.

V

JOB : II

IT is useless to argue as to the type of poem to which the Book of Job belongs. It is neither drama nor epic, in the generally accepted meanings of these terms, for there is little or no action. The nearest approach we have in the realm of dramatic literature is the Prometheus of Aeschylus—which, indeed, the poem resembles in several ways. But we have no real evidence of the existence of any drama in ancient Israel apart from the ceremonial which may have been observed at certain religious festivals in pre-exilic days. If an epic existed at all, it will have been connected with the same occasions, as it was in Accadian ritual. We must simply take the book as a dialogue in poetic form, and be content to accept it as being (if we must insist on classification) practically *sui generis*.

The dialogue is, as has been indicated, properly confined to chs. 3–27, 29–31, 38 : 1–42 : 6. The stage is already set by the prose narrative. Job has suffered and is visited by his three friends. Their origins have been much discussed, even the old story seems to have regarded them as foreigners, probably Edomites, since Edom was often held to be a home of wisdom (cf., e.g. Obad. 8). For seven days and seven nights they sat in wordless sympathy for the victim of so many disasters, and at this point the poet intervenes.

Throughout the whole dialogue, the friends adhere to the position they take up from the first. Their attitude changes, and the emotional tension grows, it is true, but there is not the slightest sign of alteration in their views or opinions. Job, on the other hand, moves forward, not in a straight line—that would be too much to expect—but by a series of approaches, each getting nearer to a fixed point, until he reaches a certain stability. This, however, does not end the debate. For Job is faced with two problems, not one. The first is wholly personal, and is concerned with his own relation to God. The second is general, and deals with the universal question of divine justice in the ordering of human affairs. The answer to the first will be a faith, the answer to the second will be a theodicy. Psychologically, it is essential that the pressure of the first should be relaxed before the poet can reach that calm of spirit which will enable him seriously to embark on the second. Half way through the debate, at the end of ch. 19, Job attains to a position whence he can proceed to the second problem. It is impossible that his own sufferings should slip out of his sight, but they are no longer a merely personal matter ; they become an illustration of the more general question, and when he summons God to appear, it is that his difficulties may be solved in both spheres. It is the development of this line of thought that we follow in reading the book.

Job's first utterance, in ch. 3, is simply a cry of pain. He asks questions, it is true, but they are simply rhetorical —why had he to be born at all ? Why, if he must be born, could he not have perished at once, as an unconscious infant or even as a still-born child ? Why, if he had to live and suffer, can he not die at once, and be rid of his misery in the drab equality of Sheol ? It is interesting to note, in passing, that the idea of suicide never occurs to Job. Indeed, it seems from the poem in general that he does not really wish to die ; rather he complains that an early death is inevitable. It is clear that the problem, as a problem, has not yet arisen.

The great question is actually raised by the speech of Eliphaz (chs. 4–5). It is one indication of the poet's high artistic level that every step Job takes has as its starting-point a remark of one of the friends. Though they never move from the position they take up at the start, they have their place in the development of Job's thought, and it is in this way that each makes his own contribution to the subject. Eliphaz appears in many ways as a really lovable character. He is an old man— older than Job's father (15 : 10), and is full of tender sympathy for his suffering friend. He has seen much of life, and yet he has a higher source of knowledge than experience. He is a mystic, one of those favoured spirits for whom the veil between the seen and the unseen is at times drawn aside. What he has to say is based on such a moment of vision, awe-inspiring yet reliable. He begins with the utmost tact, and lays his hand on the wound with great tenderness. Yet already there is a hint of irony which runs through the book. Job has often given comfort to the distressed ; can he not apply to his own case what he has administered to others ? It really is true, for Eliphaz has learnt the facts by direct revelation. And what are the facts ? Simply that every incident of suffering has its cause in human sin. It is the penalty imposed by a perfectly righteous God on all who stray, even in the least degree, from the right path. So high are the divine standards, and so perfect is the demand of God, that the very angels cannot escape criticism and condemnation. But there is no wrong without a remedy. Job must have done something, of which he himself may be unconscious, but which, nevertheless, has roused divine justice to punishment. It may be only a little matter ; let Job humble himself before God, confess that he is in fault, and throw himself on the mercy of the Omnipotent. Then all will be well. Prosperity will once more be his, he will have descendants innumerable (for we must not forget that an abundant posterity was the supreme blessing for the ancient east), and many years of peaceful happiness await him before he sinks gently into his grave at an extreme age.

Seldom has the utter futility of conventional language been more ruthlessly exposed than in this speech of Eliphaz. Job may well have spoken thus in days gone by, but now he knows that comfort of this kind is absolutely worthless. What is the use of promising a happy end to a man who knows that it is impossible ? Job is suffering from an incurable disease ; he may linger for a few years, but every moment will bring its special pain. Not only is there no hope whatever of a cure ; there is not even the slightest prospect of any alleviation. Job's children are dead, and a hundred others will not compensate for the loved ones who have been taken from him. We cannot help feeling that the poet has here the conclusion of the old story in mind. It is nonsense to suppose that the seven sons and three daughters mentioned in 42 : 13 will really make up for those who have gone, and it is this speech of Eliphaz which brings out the absurdity.

Nevertheless, Eliphaz has said something of profound importance. He has made Job realize that the author of his sufferings is none other than God Himself, and that he has somehow incurred the divine anger. At once the problem is raised in an acute form. Is God really the friend of the good ? Are his judgments fair ? Job may have done wrong, though he has taken every precaution to avoid even unconscious sins and to atone for any that may have been committed inadvertently. This he never denies. But he *knows* that he has never been guilty of an offence which is in the smallest degree commensurate with the penalty imposed by God. So his reply to Eliphaz (chs. 6–7) begins with the complaint that the friends have no real understanding of the position. If they will only tell him where his sin is, he will repent and confess, but he will not tell a lie to save himself. For a time details of his sufferings break in on his thought. This is a characteristic touch, and is liable to reappear from time to time. Racked with pain, beset by horrors, night and day, Job finds it almost impossible to think continuously along any one line, though when the spasm is over he can return to the main thread of his reasoning. At the moment, the outbreak has its place, for it leads Job to challenge God directly. Why should he, an insignificant and harmless mortal, become the special object of divine wrath? If, like the primeval chaos-monster, he had sought to wreck the universe, God's action would be intelligible and justifiable. But there can be no reason why God should fix His attention on so small a creature as Job ; we note, incidentally, the bitter parody of Ps. 8 : 4. God must be making a mistake, which He will discover some day, and then it will be too late, for Job will be in Sheol beyond His reach.

Even if we were not conscious of the appalling blasphemy involved in Job's last words, the speech of Bildad (ch. 8) would have brought it home to us. He makes a less favourable impression than Eliphaz, but this is certainly due in part to the fact that Eliphaz had not been irritated by Job's attitude. He must be a good man, kindly by nature and well-meaning ; otherwise he would not have been there at all. But while Eliphaz is the mystic, Bildad is the scholar. He is learned in the wisdom of the past, and can quote generations of old as his authority. Bildad shares with all his contemporaries the illogical belief that men of days gone by necessarily knew more than their descendants. But he has nothing to add to what Eliphaz has said ; his principles are the same as those already propounded. There are, of course, personal differences in the presentation. We have already noted the greater irritation, due in large measure to Job's heterodox language. But we must not overlook another source of annoyance which was doubtless present to the writer's mind. These three men, like Job himself, are experts in consolation. Hitherto the doctrine which they have propounded has been accepted and acknowledged ; the sufferers have allowed themselves to be comforted. What right has Job to reject the familiar ministrations of religion ? Only consummate arrogance could refuse what has always been found good enough for other people. Rarely suggested and never explicitly stated, this feeling runs as an undercurrent through all that the friends have to say after Job has replied to Eliphaz for the first time. So Bildad, while admitting the reward of submissive penitence which may yet be Job's lot, dwells much more on the doom that awaits the obdurate sinner—such as Job shews signs of being.

Yet Bildad, too, makes his positive contribution to the course of the discussion, though he is hardly conscious of the fact. At the outset he appeals to the divine righteousness, and thereby opens a fresh avenue for Job's thought. We must be careful to understand the full connotation of the term. Originally it belonged to the technical vocabulary of the law-court. The word " righteous " was employed to designate the successful litigant, the man who won his case. So, too, the common Hebrew word for " wicked " indicated the party which failed. Hence to " justify " is in the first place to give a legal decision in favour of a person. By a not unnatural transition the word came to imply also one who ought to win his suit, and we not infrequently have phrases like "justify the righteous" (e.g., Deut. 25 : 1), "justify the wicked for reward" (Is. 5 : 23). As the ethical sense developed, the term became even wider, and indicated moral and religious excellence, without respect to any legal procedure. It still, however, retained in addition its old forensic meaning, and might be used in either sense —or in both together. Now, by introducing this thought, Bildad puts a new idea into the mind of Job, and from this point onwards he is dominated by the thought of a trial at law, in which he himself is one party and God is the other. It is not always clear who is the complainant and who the defendant, and, indeed, it seems that Job himself is indifferent as to whether he brings or answers a charge. But he now gets the feeling that if he could only lay his case before God, or lay his case against God before an independent tribunal, he would be shewn to be in the right.

The thought of a law-suit, however, is not fully developed at once, as Job's first reply to Bildad (chs. 9–10) shews. One obstacle is instantly apparent ; no one else has a chance of pleading against God. Bildad has said that God is righteous, not clearly distinguishing between the legal and the ethical senses of the term. Job has to accept this view, at least in the legal sense. God is bound to win His case ; He is "righteous" in that way, for He could overwhelm His opponent utterly by His superior knowledge and power. However pure the adversary might be, God would still discover and prove evil in him. And yet Job plays with the thought ; he cannot get it out of his mind. In spite of his sufferings he begins to envisage a contest at law, till at last he realizes that the thing is hopeless, if only because his time is too short, and before the case can be decided or even heard, he himself will be beyond the reach of justice.

At this point Zophar makes his first appearance (ch. 11). He is even less attractive than either Eliphaz or Bildad. If the former is a mystic and the latter a scholar, Zophar has no resources outside himself on which to rely. Though the youngest of the three, he is the most dogmatic, and speaks entirely on his own authority. He knows what God would say, and undertakes to say it for Him. But, after all, it is only a repetition of the revelation made to Eliphaz and the lessons learned by Bildad, with rather more stress on Job's audacity in even entertaining the idea of a possible meeting with God. Zophar is harsher and more brusque than either of the others, and comes nearer than they to charging Job with direct sin. But he, too, admits—even insists—that if Job will repent and reform, all will yet be well with him.

Job's reply to Zophar (chs. 12–14), winding up, as it were, the first round of the debate, is the longest speech he has yet made. It brings out clearly the emotional tension under which the sufferer is labouring. At the moment it is the friends who are his main worry ; as comforters they are useless, and are talking down to him. Against this attitude of superiority his whole being revolts. He knows as much as they do, and is as fully aware as they of the majesty and omnipotence of God— a point which Zophar has stressed. Further, he understands the divine nature better than they do. They insist on being blind to one of the facts which Job knows best : he is innocent of any wrong great enough to explain his troubles. Job knows, too, that if he could only reach God, he could prove his case, and goes so far as to hint at a challenge to God, and to picture to himself some details of the trial scene. It does not matter who speaks first, he or God ; he is content to accept either rôle in the proceedings. Indeed, God has already, as it were, brought charges against him through the pain He has inflicted, though the accusations are still vague and formless. But once more he is overcome by the thought that his time is short. Sorrow is the common lot of man, and it ends only in death, that death which must soon be his own portion, cutting off for ever the hope of a reconciliation or of a recovery. New ideas rise in his mind. If a tree is cut down, fresh verdure may break from the stump, but for man death is the end. Is this really so ? Is there no possibility that even in Sheol God will find some means of communicating with man ? An entrancing thought, but Job will not shirk reality or take refuge in mere " wishful thinking." His doom is as certain as the enduring hills, and he will not for an instant allow himself to be beguiled by false hopes or theories.

We may pause for a moment to see where we stand at the end of this first series of speeches. On the one hand we have the friends, sure of their doctrine, and deducing from it Job's sinfulness. But they still have a certain sympathy with him, and are not prepared to proceed to open accusation. At the same time, his attitude, both to their views and to them personally, is producing an irritation which can but grow more violent as Job proceeds on his course. More and more he tends to disregard them, and he is so sunk in misery that he has no fear of worse consequences whatever he may say or do. His own position is becoming steadily more desperate. He has moved forward, it is true, but up to the present his divergences from the normal doctrine have led him only deeper into despair. He is beginning to believe that God does not really hate him, or seek to punish him excessively for some slight misdeed. This he could prove, if only he could meet God face to face on equal terms. But, wherever he looks, the way is barred. He is overwhelmed by divine omnipotence, and, even if he were not, still the day of his death is so near that hope dies. Nevertheless the thought of a reconciliation after death has entered his mind, if only to be rejected at once, and now that it has forced an entry, it will be difficult to keep it permanently from him.

When Eliphaz speaks for the second time (ch. 15), it is clear that his mood has changed. He has nothing new to offer, and confines himself to something very like abuse. Job is arrogant and in other ways sinful, shewing respect neither for man nor for God. Such a character will necessarily meet with condign punishment, and it is worth noting that Eliphaz no longer holds out hope of restoration. That stage is past, and we feel that the friends no longer have any thought of Job's repentance.

Job begins his reply (chs. 16–17) in much the same strain as Eliphaz. As far as the friends are concerned, the discussion has sunk to mutual recrimination. But Job does not dwell long on the shortcomings of the friends ; he seems to brush them aside as a minor nuisance. He turns quickly to God, and pours out his complaint. As he reviews his sufferings the heat of his spirit rises, and he grows desperate. He cannot believe that God is what the friends depict—what he himself has hitherto supposed. He is the victim of a horrible crime, and he cries out to the earth not to let his blood go unavenged. But who is to see that justice is done ? It is God who is the criminal, if current theology be correct. But this cannot be the real truth, and Job makes a vast leap of faith and appeals —to God ; to God as he knows He must be, not to God as man fancies Him to be. There is One in the heavens who will see that the right is done, and to Him Job turns his eyes and makes his plea. But, almost with the appeal, he falls back into a still deeper abyss of doubt than he has yet fathomed, for he is doomed, and there is no time for his justification before he descends into the pit of Sheol.

Bildad's second speech (ch. 18) is simply a statement of the dangers which beset the wicked, with the obvious implication that Job comes under that heading. Indeed there are hints which suggest the actual experiences through which he has passed, as, for instance, the reference to the childlessness of the sinner in v. 19. Like Eliphaz, Bildad seems no longer to contemplate the possibility of Job's repentance and restoration, and his speech is almost an imprecation, for it is couched in language even stronger than any that has been previously used by the friends.

The sting and the bitterness of Bildad's attack rouse Job to the extreme limit of desperation, and in ch. 19 he reaches the point at which something final must happen. Either he will go under altogether, or he will take some step which, however improbable it seems, will yet give him at least a measure of permanent relief. He has several times approached this point, but the nearer he has been to it, the more sudden and complete has been his relapse into hopeless misery. Now he has reached the climax. First he complains, as usual, of the treatment of the friends. Then his mind turns to God and the tortures, physical, social and spiritual, which are being inflicted on him. The thought drives him almost to madness; he cries out to the friends for pity. They are useless, and he comes back to the idea of a written document on which his words might be inscribed for future justification. Now he has reached the lowest point, and suddenly with a series of swift leaps he rises higher than he has ever done before, and finds at last a rock on which his feet may be planted.

In parts the crucial verses, 19 : 25-27, are obscure, and have given rise to much discussion. The text, too, is uncertain in the first half of v. 26. Nevertheless there are certain features of this great utterance which we may recognize with some confidence. The first is the conception of the " Goel." Much misunderstanding has been caused in English-speaking circles by the rendering of this word as " redeemer." That translation may be possible in some contexts, but even then only with a limited application. A " Goel " is the legal representative of a person who, for some reason or other, is unable to exercise the ordinary rights of citizenship. A woman often needed a " Goel," since her standing in the community was not on the same level as that of the other sex. The whole story of the Book of Ruth turns on the functions of the " Goel " in such a case. Naomi and Ruth cannot act for themselves ; Boaz (" Near kinsman " is another rendering of " Goel ") is induced to act for them. A slave, or a person dispossessed of his ancestral property, might need the services of a " Goel " to buy his freedom or to " redeem " his land. A man's highest interest normally centred in what happened to his descendants after his death, and a dead man is certainly incapable of exercising his rights ; he must have a " Goel " if there is any matter in dispute. In particular, if he has died a violent death, he himself is obviously unable to exact the penalty, and the duty devolves on the " Goel of blood " (E VV. " Avenger of blood " or " Revenger of blood ").

That is much the situation in which Job finds himself. He is as good as dead, and he is to die with his case still unproved. His right to justification remains unfulfilled during his lifetime. Some one, then, must take up the matter after he has gone, and make full use of the statement which has flitted before his eyes in v. 23. But who will do the work? His children are all dead. He has no other relatives. The friends are hostile, and, indeed, are ranged among the accusers. In this blank *impasse* his mind flies back to his audacious venture, indicated in 16 : 19, " Behold my witness is in the heavens, and he that shall testify for me is on high." It is none other than God Himself who will see justice done, and ensure that Job's essential innocence shall be proclaimed. He will stand upon the earth in time to come and will prove Himself to be Job's " Goel "—He, the eternally living One.

So far, so good. But that is not enough. Job will be satisfied by nothing less than the absolute certainty that he himself will see the consummation of his wishes and hopes. He now *knows* that God, in spite of any appearance to the contrary, is really on his side. As already remarked, the first part of v. 26 is obscure and probably corrupt—certainly there is no mention of worms, as in A.V., but the latter part of this verse and the whole of that which follows are perfectly clear " . . . and apart from my flesh I shall see God, whom I, yes, I shall behold, and my eyes see, and not another's, when my reins fail within me." We are inevitably reminded of Ps. 73 : 26, and there may be a connexion between the two passages, though it is impossible to say on which side the debt lies. But it is hardly possible to doubt that Job has at last envisaged a life after death in which he will still remain in touch with God. This is no statement of a general doctrine either of immortality or of resurrection, but it is the expression of Job's conviction that after his death God will

have justice done to him, and that somehow, apart from
his physical frame, Job will see it for himself.

All things considered, this is a very extraordinary conclusion for Job to reach.   When Pharisaic Judaism
developed a belief in life after death, the doctrine normally
took the form of resurrection, i.e., the reconstruction and
re-animation of the physical body.   The conception of an
immortal spirit, liberated for ever from the bonds of
matter, is Greek rather than Jewish.   But here and in one
or two other places, notably in Ps. 73, we seem to have
a tentative movement towards the other view.   The
characteristic Jewish psychology, which, as has been well
said, regarded man as an animated body rather than as
an imprisoned soul, carried the normal stream of belief
in life after death along other lines.   But this poet was a
pioneer, and had broken loose from all established
tradition.   It is the less surprising, then, that he should
have conceived of the future life in a form in which it
could hardly find general acceptance among his direct
successors.   But he did reach this point, and out of the
bitterness of his soul and the horror of his experience,
he formed a belief which has changed the whole outlook
of the human spirit.

True, a doctrine of immortality was found in Greece
at the end of the fifth century B.C.   It was, too, genuine
immortality, involving not merely the survival of personality after death, but an experience of all those
spiritual values which stand highest to man.   We cannot
read the *Phaedo* without feeling that in some ways the
Greek has outstripped the Hebrew in the search for divine
truth.   Yet there is one fundamental difference in the
approach by which these truths were reached.   The
Greek attained his belief in immortality through logic
and psychology, the Hebrew through his theology and

his ethic. In the one case the doctrine was based on the study of man, in the other on knowledge of God.

Job has thus reached a solution of the first of his problems. The pain is still with him, and he cannot forget his sufferings, but the stress is relieved, and the intensity of feeling is to some extent lessened. It is now possible to turn to the larger question and handle it with some degree of calmness. Needless to say, the friends entirely fail to appreciate the situation. To them Job is still merely blasphemous and arrogant, and the relief which he has experienced in unorthodox ways is but an added offence. We get a hint of this in Zophar's second speech (ch. 20). It is as violent and abusive as ever, but it lays stress on the evanescence of any pleasure or happiness which the wicked may enjoy. Here, surely, we have a reflection of what is to be seen on Job's face, the comparative calm, with a possible glint of real happiness, which comes over his expression as he attains the great height of ch. 19.

Ch. 21 begins, as usual, with an appeal to the friends. But here there is a difference. Job is clearly making a fresh start, and demands a hearing, not for a recital of his own sorrows, but for a statement of fact which will contradict the whole position taken up by the friends. It is not true that disaster always befalls the wicked. He is successful, not only in matters where his own efforts alone are required, but also in spheres which are supposed to be under the direct control of God. That means that his prosperity is a part of the divine purpose, and he may live to an advanced old age and come to the grave in peace. All this in spite of the fact that he is wicked, and that he deliberately throws God on one side, refusing to admit His rights or claims. Job is well aware of the opposition which his words will rouse in his friends, but

nevertheless he must state the facts. So the stage is set for
a discussion on the general problem of divine providence.

Eliphaz (ch. 22), however, is in no mood to discuss
general theological or philosophical questions. He is
concerned primarily to abuse Job. The first point that
strikes him is the arrogance of a man who thinks that
God has anything to gain by human goodness. Then,
failing to note the logical corollary of his remarks, which
should imply that God is also indifferent to human sin,
he launches into a catalogue of the sins which (presumably) Job has committed. They are those of the rich,
economic oppression, selfish neglect of suffering, repudia-
tion of God, and the like. Needless to say, there is no
ground, either in the old story or in the debate, for supposing that Job really has been guilty of these things.
But his disasters make it clear to Eliphaz that Job is a
sinner ; his attitude under affliction has strengthened this
belief, and this is the kind of iniquity which a man in
Job's former position would be most likely to commit.

To this attack Job (chs. 23-24) makes no direct
reply, though it would seem that the charges are kept in
mind and recalled later. But Eliphaz has brought him
back to one important point. He has suggested that Job
should seek God (22 : 23ff.), and Job desires nothing
better. He knows now that God is on his side, and the
only problem remaining is how to find Him. For a time
the difficulty appears insuperable, and Job turns from it
to formulate a statement of the case he would present if
he were able to stand in the divine presence. The text
of ch. 24 is obscure and probably corrupt in parts, but it
seems clear that it involved a description of the oppression inflicted by the wicked on the poor, and the miserable
condition of the lower classes. It is, in fact, an elabora-
tion of the position which has already been indicated

in ch. 21, and we see how readily now the personal problem is merged in the general.

We now come to a section of the book in which, as we have seen, there appears to be a certain amount of confusion in the text. Assuming the general correctness of the reconstruction attempted in the last chapter, we observe that Bildad renews and reiterates the charges which the friends have already brought against Job, especially the accusation of impiety. It must be remembered that to the ancient Hebrew the most important element in a right attitude to God lay in complete and humble submission to His will, together with a recognition of the gulf which separates the infinite from the infinitesimal. So, if 26 : 2 be really the opening of Bildad's third speech, he starts with a sarcastic question—Did Job find God weak and foolish, and aid Him with the resources of his human strength and wisdom ? Bildad answers his own question by the might of God as shown in creation, and refers to the doctrine stated at the first by Eliphaz, that no person or thing can be perfect in the sight of the Almighty. The old creation myth rises to his mind ; did not God destroy the great Chaos monster (here called Rahab), and establish the Cosmos by His own solitary power ?

Job is thus brought back to his own position. We have reason to believe that a large portion of this speech is lost. Job does not for a moment deny the power of God, but he does insist on his own essential innocence. No *argumentum ad verecundiam* can shake his conviction on that head ; facts are facts, and a theology which fails to include them in its scheme of things stands self-condemned. From the fragments which survive we may guess that Job went on to insist on the conflict between theory and reality which is manifest in the beliefs of the friends.

When Zophar speaks for the last time, it is clear that he has abandoned any attempt at argument, and has to take refuge in abuse. He sketches, apparently with vindictive glee, the misfortunes of the wicked, which so closely resemble those of Job himself, and the closing sentences form a terrible imprecation.

This is all that the friends can say or do. They have started with the intention of doing their best for the sufferer, and of giving him comfort and hope. They have felt a deep affection and even admiration for him in the past, and they are genuinely grieved by his calamities. But the only aid they can offer is that suggested by their conventional theology, and their presentation of their case has not only failed to bring relief to the sufferer, but has complicated and aggravated the agony of his soul. With his inability to accept their doctrine, and his rejection of its basic principle that all suffering is due to, and is proportionate to, human sin, their irritation at his wilfulness, arrogance and self-righteousness has steadily grown, till it has totally eclipsed their affection and sympathy, and their last word is a curse.

But now Job has done with them. Ch. 28, as we have seen, formed no part of the original poem, and it is in chs. 29–31 that Job turns to God to make his final appeal. It is inevitable that his own case, as an example of the general situation, should once more take the leading position in his thought. Ch. 29 is devoted to a summary of his former prosperity, and it is interesting to observe that what Job has valued most is not his wealth but the respect in which he was held by all about him. The contrast afforded by his present position is drawn in ch. 30, and once again there rises the old feeling that it is God who is responsible for the change. Yet the sufferer has already won the conviction that somehow God *must* be on his side, and that the trial will certainly take place. He therefore prepares for it with a great oath of purgation, which occupies ch. 31. In some ways it offers us the highest moral standard which the Old Testament presents, going far beyond the elementary provisions of the Decalogue and other pronouncements of the Law. In sexual morality it almost anticipates the position taken by Jesus Himself; Job has never looked upon a woman to lust after her. He has never assumed the full authority of the master over his slaves, for to him they have always been personalities with rights of their own—would that God might treat him in like fashion! The appeal of distress and poverty has never failed to win response from him. He has been wealthy, it is true, but has never trusted in riches. His fidelity to God has been unswerving, and no enticement has induced him to share in the heathen cults of those about him. Strict honesty has marked all his dealings with his neighbours —in short there is no one of the sins so familiar to the world to which he has surrendered himself. That is his case, and, bearing it proudly with him, he would enter the presence of his righteous Accuser and Judge.

For the response to this appeal the reader of our present text has to wait till Elihu has said his say. But, as we have seen, in its original form the poem probably had no reference to the fourth friend, and we may pass on at once to ch. 38. It is introduced with a sentence which may well have been taken from the last scene of the popular tale. A storm-cloud has gathered on the horizon while Job and the friends have been talking, and now, from the black dome of whirling cloud, Yahweh Himself speaks. At last we are to have the answer to Job's questions and the justification of his position.

But, strangely enough, there is no answer. God begins

in language very like that which the friends have used.
Job is not as wise as he had supposed. In swift succession the marvels and mysteries of the physical universe
are brought before him. His mind is turned to the
structure of the world, with its limitless variety in earth,
sea and sky. But this is not all, for the cosmos has not
merely been created ; its endless movements have been
maintained and controlled. Man may have tamed
some of the beasts and brought them to do his will, but
even these he does not fully understand, and there are
countless others of whose life he knows and cares nothing.
What is Job that he should argue with the Creator and
Sustainer of all this, or pit his scanty knowledge against
the Omniscient ?

What strikes us most in the divine speeches is that they
contain nothing that is fundamentally new. The position
has been stated by the friends, though less forcibly, and
has been admitted by Job. It did not solve the intellectual problem then, and at first sight it is not clear
why it should do so now. Indeed, had the theophany been
granted to Job at an early stage in the development of his
thought, we may well suspect that it would merely have
enhanced his sense of rebellious despair. But much has
happened since the debate began. Above all Job has
reached the conviction that God is essentially friendly.
Though His words may be harsh and His rebuke severe,
there is yet the certainty that He will grant fair treatment.
Further, there is a vast difference between a picture of
God presented by a weak and ignorant mortal and the
same picture drawn by God himself. As Job says, he
had heard of God with the hearing of the ear, but now his
eye seeth Him. Hitherto, so to speak, He has been asked
to accept knowledge of God at second hand ; now He
knows what He is like from direct communication.

What is the result of all this? Only one issue is possible to the mind of the ancient east, and Job falls in utter self-abasement at the feet of God, overwhelmed by a sense of his own insignificance and of the majesty of the Omnipotent. And there the poet leaves him.

It may well be said that the book offers no solution to the second of the two problems which are involved. This is true, but it does something even better than offer a solution ; it shews that a solution is not really necessary for the spiritual life of man. Job has forgotten all about his problems ; for him they have ceased to exist. All his sufferings have fallen into the background, and all his desperate struggles have ceased. He has seen God and heard His voice. Nothing else is now of the slightest importance, for in the vision of the Infinite the finite may rest with humility, submission, and confidence. Had music and not poetry been the author's art he would have endorsed the utterance of Browning's organist :

" Sorrow is hard to bear, and doubt is slow to clear ;
    Each sufferer says his say, his scheme of the weal and woe ;
    But God has a few of us whom He whispers in the ear,
    The rest may reason and welcome, 'tis we musicians know."

VI

THE PSALMS : I

THE Hebrew Psalter holds a unique position in the religious literature of mankind. It has been the hymn-book of two great religions, and has expressed their deeper spiritual life through the centuries. It has ministered to men and women of widely different races, languages and cultures. It has brought comfort and inspiration to the sorrowing and to the faint-hearted in all ages. Its words have shewn themselves to be adaptable to the needs of people who have no knowledge of its original form and little understanding of the conditions under which it was produced. No other part of the Old Testament has exercised so wide, so deep, or so permanent an influence on the life of the human soul. Ancient Mesopotamia, Egypt and Greece had their hymns, often of great beauty and power, while Hinduism (or rather the Vedic ancestor of Hinduism) had an immense corpus of religious poetry. But the earlier faiths have passed away, leaving their literature for the investigation of the specialist ; Hinduism was never more than the religion of one race and country, and its noblest utterances often came in practice to be used as little more than magic formulae. Buddhism and Islam, the only two religions which have shared with Christianity a claim to universal adherence, are not distinguished for their religious poetry. The Book of Psalms stands alone in its permanence and in its universality.

But while, through the ages, this little collection of a

hundred and fifty poems has taken and held its place, and has ministered to countless human spirits, it is still worth while examining its structure and history, if only that we may catch something of the divine method of revelation. Naturally no formal record of the process whereby the Psalter reached its present form has come down to us, and we are compelled to rely on such evidence as the book itself affords. There is, however, a good deal that may be gathered from its pages as to its history. For it is clear that it had a history, and this is only what we should expect. It is included in the third section of the Hebrew Bible, and, though it stands at the head of that section, it is clear that its canonicity was recognized at a later period than that of the Law or the Prophets. Individual Psalms may well have undergone modification as succeeding generations adapted their words to special needs and circumstances. This is a common experience ; some of our best-known English hymns are to-day never sung in exactly the form in which they came from the author's pen. There are, further, signs of deliberate compilation, which attest the existence of earlier collections, and we have other Jewish hymns which came into existence too late to be included in the Hebrew Canon—indeed it seems probable that some of them were never written in Hebrew at all.

In the Hebrew Bible the Psalter is divided into five books :

      I.   Pss. 1—41
     II.   Pss. 42—72
   III.   Pss. 73—89
   IV.   Pss. 90—106
    V.   Pss. 107—150.

The five sections are obviously very unequal in length, and the figure five suggests an imitation of the five books of Moses. There is, further, no break of any kind between Pss. 106 and 107, such as we may see so clearly after Ps. 41, and there is further reason to suspect that the original division was into three, not five sections. This, of course, does not necessarily mean that a particular Psalm in the latter part of the book was necessarily composed later than one found in an earlier section ; indeed there are cases where a Psalm appears in more than one division.

The suggestion of an original three-fold division is supported by one very striking fact. As all careful readers of the Bible will have noticed, there are several different names applied to God in the Old Testament. Two of these are much more frequent than others, the proper name of the God of Israel, Yahweh (normally replaced in the English versions by the word LORD in small capitals), and the more general term rendered simply God. Now it is a striking fact that in nearly all the Psalms in Books II and III (more exactly in Pss. 42–83) the term Yahweh is comparatively rare, and in many does not occur at all in our present text. "God" is used alone, i.e., without a possessive pronoun or other genitive, about 200 times in the Psalter, and of these no less than about 180 instances occur in Bks. II and III. On the other hand the name Yahweh is found only 44 times in these Psalms (42–83), though it is so frequent elsewhere in the book.

It appears, too, that in many cases the poet himself used the name Yahweh, and that this has been deliberately altered to "God" by a later hand. Expressions like "Upon the harp will I praise thee, O God, my God" (Ps. 43 : 4), "God, thy God, hath anointed thee" (Ps. 45 : 7) and "I am God, thy God" (Ps. 50 : 7), though not impossible, are unnatural as compared with "Yahweh,

thy God." More convincing is evidence supplied by
"doublets," i.e., Psalms, or portions of Psalms, which are
found more than once in the Psalter. A good instance is
offered by Pss. 14 and 53, which are nearly identical.
The word Yahweh occurs four times in Ps. 14, and in
every case it is represented by "God" in Ps. 53. This,
it is true, is not the only difference between the two
Psalms, but the resemblances are so close as to make it
certain that both are editions of the same original. The
variation in the divine name, then, must be deliberate.
We are justified in believing that Pss. 42–83 once formed a
separate collection, to which Pss. 84–89 were added before
the whole was included in our present Psalter.

Another case of "doublets" may give us some further
light. Ps. 108 falls into two parts, vv. 1-5 appearing also
in Ps. 57 : 7-11, and vv. 6-13 in Ps. 60 : 5-12. The term
"God" occurs more than once in both parts, while
Yahweh is found only in Ps. 108 : 3, where it replaces,
not "God," but the Hebrew word for "Lord." This
fact would seem to indicate that Ps. 108 was compiled
from the other two in their present form, in other words
the second big collection was already in existence when
the third was put together.

We do not know at what period or for what reasons the
change of the divine name was made in Pss. 42–83.
There was, from the third century B.C. onwards, a strong
feeling in some Jewish quarters that the name Yahweh
should never be pronounced, even in reading the Scrip-
tures, lest it should be inadvertently "taken in vain."
So the translators, who in the third century B.C. began the
production of a Greek Bible for the use of Jews living in
Egypt and elsewhere, always substituted the word
"Lord," and their example has been followed by most
other versions, ancient and modern. Even in the normal

reading of the Law and other parts of the Bible among Jews the Hebrew word for "Lord" was used instead of the name Yahweh. We do not know when this practice began; it seems to have been later than the Samaritan schism, but was earlier than the invention of vowel signs for Hebrew writing. (As long as Hebrew was spoken as the vernacular of Palestine no vowels were indicated, the consonants alone sufficing to give the meaning, as in modern reporters' shorthand). It may have been some such religious scruple as this which prompted the change in the central portion of the Psalter, but in that case it is not easy to see why the change was confined to this group. Another suggestion is that the collection was made, not in Palestine, but in some other country, where a copy might easily fall into heathen hands and be in some way maltreated or defiled. The divine name must not be exposed to this risk. The evidence offered by the LXX may be held to suggest an Egyptian origin for the practice. Even in Judea there were times when dangers of this kind were to be feared, especially during the oppressive reign of Antiochus Epiphanes in the middle of the second century B.C. But this is rather a late age to which to attribute the collection, and we have to admit that we can no longer recover either the motives which led to the alteration or the period in which it originated.

It seems, then, reasonable to suppose that Pss. 42–83 once formed an independent collection of sacred poems, Pss. 84–89 being added at a later period to form our present second and third books. Can we go further, and find other, possibly earlier, collections? We may note at once that there are several groups of Psalms which seem to have within themselves certain resemblances. Thus Pss. 120–134 are described in the Bible itself as "Songs of Ascents" (AV "Degrees"). This probably implies that these were especially used by pilgrims on their way up to Jerusalem, or to the Temple itself, and the fact that they all stand together suggests that they once formed an independent unity. Another group consists of Psalms to which the phrase " Hallelujah " (AV. " Praise ye the Lord ") is prefixed. These are Pss. 111–114, 116–118, 135, 136, 146–150. In some the Hallelujah stands at the end of a Psalm, but the text of the LXX suggests that it really belongs to the head of the next Psalm. This is not so compact a group as the preceding, but it is noticeable that all appear in the last of the five books, and that they do tend to run together. Here, again, we may have an original collection which has been absorbed into the larger whole.

It is also widely felt that the personal names which appear in the " titles " to the Psalms are significant in this respect. These " titles " are printed in small type in our English Bibles, and are not included in the verse enumeration, but in the Hebrew Bible they are regarded as integral parts of the Psalm, and are often counted as the first verse, though the shorter titles are sometimes merged in v. 1. Thus, for example, in Ps. 42 the words " As the hart panteth after the waterbrooks " with which the Psalm proper opens, count as v. 1 in the English versions, but as v. 2 in the Hebrew text. The result is that we often have a double verse enumeration, and many modern books on the Psalms give both, the Hebrew verse-number being added to the English in brackets. Now the commonest feature of these " titles " is the presence of a personal name, that of David being the most frequent. For many centuries the name was thought to indicate traditional authorship, but in view of the fact that Psalms bearing the same name appear to come from widely separated periods in the long history of the Old Testament, it is now more generally held among Bible students that the names indicate collections from which the Psalms in question were taken—just as the term " Sankey's hymns " is often applied to a number of hymns which were not written by Ira D. Sankey, though they were included in the collections which bear his name.

The following Psalms bear the name of David : 3–9, 11–32, 34–41, 51–65, 68–70, 86, 101, 103, 108–110, 122, 124, 131, 133, 138–145, making a total of 73 in all—practically half the Psalter. The solidarity of Bk. I is even more nearly complete than appears from this numeration, for Pss. 1 and 2 are clearly introductory, while there is little doubt that originally Pss. 9 and 10 were one. They are treated as a single Psalm in the old versions, and there is an acrostic which runs right through both Psalms. As a matter of fact, Ps. 33 is the only obtrusive Psalm in the whole of Bk. I, and it is easy to understand why a piece of this quality should be inserted with others bearing the name of Israel's most famous poet. It is not too much to conjecture that originally these thirty-seven Psalms once formed a single collection.

The remaining Davidic Psalms do not form so compact a group, though in Bk. II we have a series of twenty Psalms of which only two (and those consecutive) do not bear the name of David. There is an interesting note at the end of Ps. 72, which itself is ascribed to Solomon, saying " The prayers of David, the son of Jesse, are ended." This looks very much like the conclusion of a book or collection, and we are tempted to seek a group of Psalms bearing this special title. As a matter of fact, there are only three : Pss. 17 and 86 have it in the form " A prayer of David," while Ps. 142 has the words in the other order, ". . . of David ; a prayer." It will be noted that one of the three is included in the first Davidic collection, but, like other Psalms, it may have been in more than one, and we are still left with the possibility that there was once a collection called " The Prayers of David." The presence of Ps. 142 among the number makes it possible that this collection has been used by the compilers of the last four books, who tended to scatter them, and did not think it necessary to record the fact that the word " prayer " was included in the title of most of them.

Two other names may be considered. The first of these is " The Sons of Korah," found at the head of Pss. 42, 44–49, 84, 85, 87, 88. It should be noted that Pss. 42 and 43 are really a single poem, which has been divided into two. There are thus two groups, into the second of which a Davidic Psalm has been inserted. Again, the natural suggestion is that these eleven are taken from a single collection. In I Chron. 6 : 22 we have a certain Korah, son of Kohath, mentioned among the Levites who were responsible for the music of the tabernacle in David's time and of the Temple after it was built. There may have been a number of other collections bearing the names of distinguished musicians of the past.

In I Chron. 6 : 39 we find a certain Asaph, who is given a special position according to I Chron. 15 : 17, 19, 16 : 5, where he holds a place comparable to that of the leader of the orchestra. His name stands at the head of twelve Psalms, Pss. 73–83 and Ps. 50. It is worth noting that the three smaller collections, the second of David, the Sons of Korah, and Asaph, are mainly included in Bks. II and III, which, as we have seen, were probably at one time an independent unity. We observe, further, that the Davidic Psalms in this section tend to have much longer titles than those found elsewhere ; the

annotator often tries to identify the occasion for which
these Psalms were composed, or for which they would
have been especially suitable.

There are several other personal names in these titles.
Solomon is mentioned twice, in Pss. 72 and 127. Ps. 90
is " A prayer of Moses, the man of God." A certain
Heman the Ezrahite appears at the head of Ps. 88,
though this Psalm also belongs to the Korahite group,
and the following, Ps. 89, bears the name of Ethan the
Ezrahite. These last two occur in I Chron. 2 : 6,
where they are included in the families of Judah. Two
famous wise men are compared with Solomon (to their
disadvantage) in I Ki. 4 : 31 ; their names are Ethan
the Ezrahite and Heman. In I Chronicles a Heman and
an Ethan are mentioned alongside of Asaph (e.g. I Chron.
15 : 19), but they are not called Ezrahites, and the
additional word is probably due to confusion with the
Ethan of I Ki. 4 : 31. In any case, it does not seem
wholly probable that any one of these four gave his name
to a collection of Psalms ; the apocryphal book known as
the Psalms of Solomon is of much later date than anything in the Hebrew Psalter, and was almost certainly
written originally in Greek.

It is held in some quarters that other words in the titles
were intended to indicate the collections from which the
several pieces were taken. We find different words
describing the poems ; the simplest of these is the word
" Song," which we find at the head of a number of
Psalms. Often it is qualified in one way or another.
Thus in the " title " of Ps. 45 we have " a song of love(s)."
The phrase " Song of Ascents," appearing in Pss. 120-
134 has already been noted. In a few instances the
occasion for which a Psalm was especially adapted is
attached, e.g., Ps. 30 is described as " A song for the

dedication of the house," and Ps. 92 as " A song for the Sabbath day."

The most frequent term in this class is the word rendered " Psalm," which occurs no less than fifty-seven times. It is derived from a root which is used of instrumental music, especially in reference to some stringed instrument, and the rendering " Psalm " (from a Greek word meaning " to play on a harp ") is nearly an exact representation of the original sense. The use of the word throws an interesting light on Hebrew musical practice, but it does not seem clear why it should have been applied to a special group of Psalms. Probably most of them were sung in worship to an instrumental accompaniment, and, though wind instruments were employed, the strings clearly held a more prominent place.

Two other terms are generally interpreted as indicating some special character in the Psalms to which they are attached. Neither is very common. " Maschil " appears only thirteen times, and is usually explained as implying " pious meditation." The root, however, occurs more often in the sense of " dealing wisely " or " prudently," as in Is. 52 : 13. Either meaning would suit the Psalms to which the word is prefixed, and here, as in so many instances, we have to confess that the real meaning is no longer exactly ascertainable.

Six Psalms (16, 56–60) have the word " Michtam " in the " title." This is normally connected with a root meaning " gold," and these Psalms (which are all of unusual beauty, even for the Psalms), are regarded as " jewel pieces." The same word is used in the heading to the hymn ascribed to Hezekiah in Is. 38 : 9-20, and said to have been composed by that king on his recovery from sickness.

Next to the word " Psalm," the most frequent term employed in these " titles " is that rendered in the English Bible as " To " (R.V. ' For ') " the Chief Musician " which occurs in fifty-five Psalms. It may be noted that the preposition used is the same as that translated " of " when prefixed to a personal name. The exact meaning has been disputed ; other suggestions are " in regard to the musical rendering," and " for propitiation." But the general tendency is to retain the older explanation, and to regard the word as implying some kind of relation to the Precentor or Choirmaster.

The words just given have all been held to indicate that there were once separate collections or hymn books, bearing the titles, and that the compilers of our present Book of Psalms recorded the source or sources from which their pieces were taken. There is, however, no other evidence to support the suggestion in any one of these instances ; and in none of them is the case so strong as it is with the " Elohistic " Psalter and with those bearing personal names. We cannot deny the possibility that such collections once existed, but we can hardly speak even of probability.

As far, then, as we can ascertain, the general history of the Psalter seems to be much as follows. At various times, in most cases if not in all after the Exile, collections of hymns were made, and were given special titles connecting them with some of the best known of Israel's historical poets and musicians. Apparently these collections were four in number, two bearing the name of David, one that of Asaph and one that of the Sons of Korah. Other isolated names—Moses, Solomon, Heman and Ethan—are less likely to indicate separate collections, though the possibility cannot be absolutely denied. The first of the Davidic collections retained its identity, perhaps owing to its length, but the others were used by a compiler who included in his collection a number of poems derived from other sources, though there is little to suggest that these were taken from other collections. This group passed through the hands of people who, for some reason which we cannot certainly explain, changed the divine name Yahweh wherever it occurred, normally substituting the common term " God." The alteration may, of course, have been due to the compiler himself, or it may have been made later. The evidence suggests that possibly this compilation was used in Egypt. A third compilation was made from miscellaneous sources, which included one of the Davidic collections. The three were put together, and, finally, the second and third were each divided into two, making a total of five books.

But it was not only the book as a whole which had a history. Some of the Psalms themselves passed through changes, especially where they were much loved and used. In some instances, we can see clearly that two Psalms, or portions of two Psalms, were put together to form a new whole. This was done even at an early stage, for we find cases in the first Davidic collection. It is difficult to believe, for example, that Ps. 24 : 1-6 and 7-10 were originally composed as a single whole, for the two parts differ in style, metre and subject matter. Ps. 40, again, is composite ; vv. 1-11 and 13-17 were originally independent. Indeed the latter occurs by itself as Ps. 70. There is one interesting feature in Ps. 40 ; the compiler who combined the two portions apparently inserted v. 12 to form a link between the two parts. Others occur in later books, e.g. Ps. 108 is a combination of Ps. 57 : 7-11 with Ps. 60 : 5-12. Ps. 68 is a cento of verses derived from other poems, many of which are still extant.

Sometimes we can trace the history of a single Psalm. We may take Ps. 46 as an example. Originally it con-

sisted of three equal stanzas each having six 2 : 2 lines.
Thus the middle one runs (text slightly modified as in
LXX) :

> A river ! its streams
>   Gladden a city ;
> God has sanctified
>   His dwelling on high.
> God is in her midst ;
>   She shall *not* be moved ;
> God shall help her
>   At the turn of the morning.
> Nations are in tumult,
>   Kingdoms are moved ;
> He has uttered his voice,
>   Earth is melting.

Even this, however, is not likely to have been the original
form, since the Psalm is included in the Elohistic section,
and therefore the word God is probably a substitute for
the proper name Yahweh. A later generation found the
Psalmist's words peculiarly applicable to its need, and its
experience led it to break out at the end of each stanza
into a triumphant refrain :

> Yahweh of Hosts is with us,
> The God of Jacob is our refuge.

The occurrence of the name Yahweh in this refrain makes
it almost certain that this was a later addition. But the
process was not yet complete. The third stanza calls on
men to see Yahweh at work, not this time in catastrophic
natural phenomena, but in the realm of history. Readers,
however, had been so impressed with what had gone
before that one inserted the 3 line " what desolations he
hath wrought in the earth." This is as much out of place
as an extra 8-syllabled line would be in a " short metre "
hymn. One or two other changes were made, probably
by accidents in copying, and two lines (the last in stanza
I and the second in stanza III) are now shorter than the

rest, probably through the unintentional omission of a word or two. And the refrain has somehow dropped out after the first stanza. A history of this kind helps us to see how much ancient Israel valued, loved and used these poems of the religious life.

It will also be readily apparent that it is, in most instances, extremely difficult to assign to individual Psalms the dates of their original composition. As long as it was held that the personal names in the titles were intended to indicate authorship, the problem had often an easy solution. But since that view has been largely abandoned, we have been thrown back almost entirely on internal evidence, and this is seldom decisive. From time to time we come across points which might serve as indications of date, but as a rule references to historical events are couched in general terms, and it is difficult to pin them down to a specific occasion. Thus Ps. 74 clearly refers to the desolation of the holy city and temple by an enemy. But the sanctuary suffered on more than one occasion. Was the Psalm composed early in the exile, shortly after the desolation wrought by the armies of Nebuchadrezzar? Certainly the burning of the Temple (v. 7) would fit the year 586 B.C. But v. 8, with its mention of " places where men meet with God throughout the land " suggests a time when some kind of worship was practised at numerous centres. The phrasing appears to be so chosen as to exclude the " high places," and we get the impression that synagogues are in view. Now we have no clear evidence of synagogue worship in Palestine at least before the time of Ezra, and the sort of persecution implied is naturally associated with the Maccabaean era—say 168–165 B.C. As against this there is nothing in the historical records to show that Antiochus Epiphanes or his officers ever burnt the whole Temple. In 351 B.C.

the Phoenicians revolted against Artaxerxes III (Ochus), and the Jews were involved. They were heavily punished, and thousands were carried into captivity. There is, however, nowhere any mention of damage done to the Temple. But details are very scanty, and some scholars take refuge in this obscurity and suppose that the Psalm was composed at this period. But it is at least possible that it was developed from a nucleus which belonged to the earlier destruction of the Temple in 586.

Pss. 42–43, again, appear to have some definite historical reference (It is probably unnecessary to remark that these two were originally a single Psalm). The writer had held a position of some prominence in the religious life of the country. He had been, or was being, carried into exile, and the route lay through the lower hills of the Hermon range, where, as a matter of fact, he had nearly been drowned in a pool at the foot of some waterfall. The Temple was still standing, and he hoped some day to return to the old worship. The conditions are satisfied by the deportation of the best people in the land by Nebuchadrezzar, 596 B.C. But it is also possible that here too we have a record of experiences undergone by one of the captives of 351 B.C. It may plausibly be argued that the Psalmist's belief in the limitation of God to the Jerusalem Temple favours the earlier date, but at best this consideration offers only probability and not certainty.

There may be instances in which we can be practically certain of the occasion which called for a particular Psalm. One of the most obvious is Ps. 137. Here we have a Babylonian exile, together with special hatred against Edom, and intense bitterness towards the Chaldean empire. Taken together these points indicate fairly clearly a captivity under Nebuchadrezzar, though there is nothing which enables us to decide as between 596 and 586 B.C. ; the writer does not tell us whether the Temple is still standing or not.

Uncertainty as to dating or historical circumstances, however, matters less in studying the Psalms than in dealing with most books. True, we need to remember that there are elements in the thought of various poets which growing knowledge of God has superseded or sublimated. It must help us to eliminate the merely occasional and temporal if we could definitely put ourselves into a Psalmist's position, stand where he stood, share his experiences and see life just as he saw it. But much of this work can be done simply by reference to the Psalter itself, and what really matters about the book is that it mirrors thoughts and feelings which are common to all ages in history. Human nature is still human nature, and human needs recur age after age. The twentieth century A.D. has seen sacred buildings destroyed by fire, cities desolated by enemy action, and masses of men and women deported into practical slavery. Problems of the spirit still trouble us, and we can understand them only when we enter into the sanctuary of God. The fool still says in his heart that there is no God, and the cynic still demands " Who will shew us any good." The sense of futility and frustration still leads men to cry out that the work of their hands may be established. To-day, as in pre-Christian centuries, there are those who are ready to bless the Lord and forget not all His benefits, men and women who have found that the Lord is their shepherd, devout souls who dwell in the secret place of the Most High, and abide under the shadow of the Almighty. Not a few, having faced all the toil and anguish of life and its problems, even now find that their true happiness lies in their nearness to God, and in face of death itself they know that He is their portion for ever.

VII

THE PSALMS : II

As we have seen, it is usually impossible to assign a date
to the original composition of a Psalm. We are on surer
ground when we approach the question of the purpose
for which Psalms were composed and the way in which
they were used. It is clear that the 150 which have been
preserved in our present book are very far from exhausting the total of religious poems produced by Israel during
the periods when the Psalter was growing. Not only are
there occasional poems in the prose books, but from time
to time we have true Psalms embedded in the prophetic
writings. Nah. 1 : 2-11 is a portion of a Psalm. A whole
hymn is to be found in Hab. 3, and there are signs which
suggest that it was taken from an existing collection.
In Is. 38 : 9-20 we have a Psalm of thanksgiving ascribed
to Hezekiah. Is. 12 consists of two little Psalms, and
there are others in different prophetic books. It is clear,
then, that in our present Psalter we have an *anthology*, a
sort of Hebrew *Golden Treasury*. But, whereas in a
classical or modern anthology the poems are selected for
their literary qualities, in the Psalms of the Old Testament we feel that some other motive must have been at
work, for the pieces here preserved vary greatly in purely
literary value. We can have little doubt that the purpose
of the compilers was religious, not secular or even artistic.

Within the sphere of religion, however, there are many
forms and types of experience, and it may be assumed
that each of our Psalms was written with a view to one or

more of these. Some are frankly didactic or meditative. In such a Psalm as Ps. 91 we have sketched for us in beautiful language the contrast between the reward of righteousness and the penalty of wickedness. Sometimes the poet allows us to follow him through his struggles with one or other of those great problems which still vex the human heart. The writer of Ps. 73, for example, like the great poet whose work is enshrined for us in the Book of Job, had faced the question of suffering and its distribution, and takes us through his own spiritual battle. In Ps. 19 : 7-14, and still more obviously in Ps. 119, we have expressed the praise of the Law, and its value for human life and thought. But for the most part we may expect to find that the Psalms preserved in this book had some relation to the cultus, i.e., to the actual worship of Israel. It is especially from this point of view that modern students approach the study of the Psalter.

In order to determine as nearly as possible the place that each Psalm took in the religious life of the people, there are two or three indications which may be taken into account. In the " titles " of a few Psalms we have mention of some special occasion for which the Psalm is particularly suited. Thus Ps. 92 is assigned to the Sabbath, and was used in the special ritual for that day. At the head of Ps. 30 we have the phrase " for the dedication of the house," and it is natural to think of the reconsecration of the Temple by Judas Maccabaeus. No doubt the Psalm was used on this occasion, and on the annual celebrations which followed and are still maintained. Sometimes the contents of a Psalm suggest its suitability for a special occasion. Pss. 3 and 4, for example, are companion pieces ; while both imply a time of difficulty and danger, the former belongs to the morning and the latter to the evening.

It is comparatively seldom, however, that we are able to identify an occasion so clearly as we can in the cases just cited. It is possible, on the other hand, in a number of cases, to get some idea of the place a Psalm may have taken in the service itself. Here it is useful to note the class or type to which a poem belongs. The elucidation of these types we owe in the main to Gunkel, who identifies a number of classes, including the following :

1. " Hymns," or Songs of Praise.
2. Laments of the Community.
3. Royal Psalms.
4. Laments of the Individual.
5. Thanksgiving of the Individual.

These are the largest classes, and to them are added smaller groups :

6. Blessings and Curses.
7. Pilgrim Psalms.
8. Thanksgiving of Israel.
9. Legends.
10. Psalms of the Law.
11. Prophetic Psalms.
12. " Wisdom " Psalms.

There are also Psalms in which the types are mixed, Psalms in which the character is changed as the Psalm progresses, and Psalms which in themselves are short liturgies.

Now most of these types are easily recognizable, and several have a quite definite form. The first class, for example, commonly begins with an invocation or a call to praise. The singer (who may be either an individual or the community as a whole) calls on others to offer praise, or expresses his own determination to celebrate the goodness and greatness of Yahweh. One of the most

familiar is Ps. 100, which summons all the earth to make a
joyful noise before Yahweh. In Pss. 96 and 98, again, the
worshippers are exhorted to sing a new song. In Ps. 95
there is a slight modification, the exhortation being in
the first person " Let us sing." Ps. 103 opens with the
poet's appeal to his own soul to bless Yahweh ; a general
exhortation comes at the end.

This introductory demand for worship is followed by a
statement of the grounds on which it is made. These
may be general, national, or individual. Thus Ps. 96 is an
appeal to all nations to recognize that it is Yahweh alone
who is their God. The reasons given in this piece are not
elaborated ; Yahweh is great and praiseworthy, and will
eventually judge the whole earth. Sometimes the Psalmist begins his ascription of praise without an introductory
appeal. Ps. 8, for instance, simply opens " O Yahweh
our Lord, how excellent is thy name in all the earth,"
and then goes straight on with a short list of the great
deeds that Yahweh has done. A typical illustration of
the national type may be found in Ex. 15, which certainly
comes under the head of " Psalm," though it is not
included in the Psalter. In Ps. 103, again, the benefits
recited are those conferred on the individual, though,
here as elsewhere, it is always possible to interpret the
individual as being the whole community.

Not a few of these hymns of praise may also be assigned
to others of Gunkel's classes. Thus Ps. 134 is included
among the Pilgrim Psalms, though it consists simply of an
exhortation to praise Yahweh. Thanksgiving Psalms,
too, are naturally allied to songs of praise. What gives
them their specific character is that they contain phrases
which suggest that they had a definite setting in the actual
cultus, and were used in the ritual of one or other of the
various forms of thankoffering. We may take Ps. 116 as a

typical case. It is the utterance of one who has been grievously sick, and has made a vow for his recovery. On being restored to health, he comes to the Temple, to fulfil his vow and to make public acknowledgment of his obligation to God. There is a ritual method which has to be followed ; it includes the question " what shall I render unto Yahweh ? " and the answer, probably in the first instance put into the mouth of the directing priest, " I will take the cup of salvation." Apparently the formal proceedings involved the draining of a special cup. Here we have something like a small liturgy. Ps. 32, again, has a liturgical form. The worshipper, having suffered from sickness which he attributes to his sin, has confessed, and his recovery shows him that he has been forgiven. This he states, again, apparently in public, and his admission of benefit is followed by an exhortation addressed to him. The words are clearly those of Yahweh Himself, but they were probably communicated through the priest.

A special type of " Hymn " is what is sometimes called the " enthronement " Psalm. This is not to be confused with the " Royal " Psalms, which deal with a human monarch. But a divine kingship was widely recognized in the ancient east, and in one instance, that of Ammon, the national god was known as " the King." Recent studies in Semitic religion have made it clear that in many parts of the Nearer East there was an annual ceremonial at which the national deity was enthroned. The ritual was often elaborate, and included a dramatic representation of the acts of creation and a divine marriage which ensured fertility and prosperity for the following year. There are good reasons for supposing that such a ritual was performed in pre-exilic Israel, though, as it probably contained features repugnant to the high Israelite moral sense, references to it have been almost entirely suppressed in our surviving literature. If it existed, it was probably connected with the Feast of Tabernacles, which, in pre-exilic days marked the beginning of the year. The ceremonial probably involved the recitation and dramatic representation of a Creation story not unlike that which we find in Mesopotamia, and appropriate hymns would be sung as Yahweh ascended His throne after His triumph over the powers of Chaos and death. They assumed that Yahweh's reign had already begun, but, since it is obvious that the ideal age has not yet arrived, these songs necessarily had an eschatological element in them. A good illustration of this type may be seen in the second part of Ps. 24 : " Lift up your heads, O ye gates . . .", which is clearly suitable for a point in the ceremonial at which the newly crowned divine king is about to enter the sanctuary which is to be His abode for the coming year. Several of them begin " Yahweh is King ! ", e.g., Pss. 93, 97, 99. cf. also Pss. 47 : 2, 95 : 3, 96 : 10. We note further the demand for a " new song " at the opening of Pss. 96 and 98. If modern scholarship is right in associating Psalms of this type with an enthronement festival, we may be thankful that this part of the ritual has survived, and that it can be given an eternal significance.

We turn now to the second of the main classes, the Laments of the Community. These are especially appropriate to the ritual of fast-days. The people have suffered some frightful calamity, or are in terrible danger. They inevitably attribute their misfortunes to the anger of Yahweh, and are sometimes at a loss to know what has aroused it. They have, accordingly, " afflicted their souls " in a public fast, and are gathered to give expression to their penitence and their request. The most conspicuous Psalms in this group are Pss. 44, 74, 79, 80 and 83. It is interesting to note how often the worshippers refer to the great things Yahweh has done for His people in the past, cf. Pss. 44 : 1f, 74 : 2, 13ff., 80 : 8-11, 83 : 9. But for the most part they consist of a recital of the disasters which have befallen the nation and a prayer for deliverance. The sufferers stress the fact that Yahweh is their God, and for His own sake He is urged to help them. It is clear to them that their troubles (usually the triumph of a ruthless enemy) are due to the anger of Yahweh, but they cannot understand what they have done to incur His displeasure. It is noticeable that in none of the five typical Psalms mentioned is there any hint of repentance, even that general penitence which Psalmists sometimes profess for sins of which they are not conscious. On the other hand we may get protestations of innocence, as in Ps. 44 : 8, 18. There is no attempt at an intellectual solution of the problem, such as we have, for example, in the Book of Job ; there is simple bewilderment and a plea that Yahweh will put forth His power once more and save His chosen people.

The class to which the name of " Royal Psalms " has been given includes pieces of varied character. All, however, are concerned with a king, and it may be assumed that the reference is to a king of Judah. Indeed, we find David mentioned from time to time, and an appeal made to the promises given to the founder of the Jerusalem dynasty. While, then, some may have undergone modification in the course of transmission, in their original form all are to be regarded as pre-exilic. Under this head Gunkel classes Pss. 2, 18, 20, 21, 45, 72, 101, 110, 132, 144 : 1-11.

Most of these seem to refer to times of special need, particularly to the eve of a military expedition or a battle.

Such are Pss. 2, 20, 110, 144 : 1-11. Ps. 45 is a marriage ode, and Ps. 72 is clearly suited to the accession of a monarch. In some cases we can see an obvious liturgical arrangement. In Ps. 20, for instance, we have at the outset a prayer uttered by the officiating priest, through whom, presumably, the king has offered his petition. This is followed, apparently, by an interval, during which some sign is manifest, and in v. 6 the king, having received the assurance that he seeks, breaks out " Now I know . . ." Ps. 2 gives a quotation of the divine decree of appointment, and we may well suppose that its enunciation formed an element in the service for which this piece was designed. A similar pronouncement appears in Ps. 110, and others in Ps. 132. In Ps. 144, again, we have an opening prayer, and then in v. 9 comes an outburst of thanksgiving for a victory which is assured if not already achieved. Here, too, we shall understand the spirit of the Psalm best if we suppose that the officiating priest did or said something in the name of Yahweh which gave the required assurance.

Some of these Psalms are more general in their application. Ps. 18 is a song of gratitude after a great victory ; Ps. 21 is an expression of the monarch's needs. Enemies are mentioned, but there is no special stress on the perils of war, and other aspects of royal life are equally contemplated. We have already observed the particular application of Pss. 45 and 72 ; Ps. 132 looks as if it belonged to a special temple ceremony in which the king took a prominent part, perhaps in connection with the New Year celebrations. We can understand why it is included in the " Songs of Ascents."

The Laments of the Individual form a large class, probably the largest of all. There has been a good deal of discussion on the question as to whether these really are personal, or whether the "I" who makes his complaint is not rather the whole people of Israel personified as a single unit. Here it is enough to remark that while this explanation may be suitable to a number of these Psalms, there are others to which it appears inapplicable. In such a piece as Ps. 32 the cry of the heart is so clear that we can hardly avoid taking it as the expression of an individual need. And there are smaller groups within the larger whole, such as those which are adapted for the fulfilment of vows and those which have a forensic interest, which can scarcely be assigned to the community as a whole. The seven so-called "Penitential Psalms" (6, 32, 38, 51, 102, 130, 143) may be taken as typical, though Ps. 130 seems to have been adapted for the use of the nation as a whole by the addition of the last two verses. In general these Psalms are of much the same character as the laments of the community. They do not, however, appeal so frequently to the great things Yahweh has done in the past, nor do they represent that it will be to His credit to rescue his afflicted servant. We do, however, sometimes meet with an arrangement which suggests some kind of liturgy—the presentation of the case followed by the assurance that the prayer will be granted. This is especially notable where the suffering endured is attributed by the worshipper to his own wrongdoing. He confesses that he has sinned, and pleads for forgiveness, being met with the answer that his iniquity has been removed. Prayers of this kind may well have been associated with the sin-offering. The actual offence is never described, a circumstance which would fit in well with the view that they are forms of prayer to be used on many different occasions. Not that this in any way detracts from the intensity of the feeling, the reality of the sense of sin, or the genuineness of repentance.

The Psalms were, one and all, originally the work of men who had been through what they describe, and have left on record an experience which may be of wide application. After all, sin, suffering, repentance, forgiveness— these are common to all religions and to all men who have any religious outlook.

Quite a number of these Psalms have special reference to sickness. Outstanding among these is Ps. 32, whose author had clearly been the victim of some violent fever, which had brought him to the very gates of death. He took the view that this disaster was the direct punishment for some sin, confessed, and saw in his recovery the complete justification of this theory. He came to the sanctuary to acknowledge all that he had received and to make public profession of his gratitude. We cannot escape the feeling that we have here too some kind of liturgical formula. After the statement of the case the Psalmist makes an appeal to all who are in right relations with Yahweh to join in his act of worship. Then the speaker suddenly changes, and we have the words of Yahweh Himself. The divine response is, of course, communicated by a member of the sanctuary staff, either priest or, possibly, prophet. The worshipper is assured of Yahweh's guidance and instruction, and warned that he must henceforth shew himself submissive and obedient. In conclusion the worshipper again speaks himself, declaring in general terms his certainty of divine deliverance, and once more calling on all the righteous and upright to burst into praise.

In Ps. 32 : 7 there is a vague reference to an " adversary " (E VV " trouble "). He plays no particular part in this Psalm, but in others he is more prominent. It is not clear at first sight who he is, and how he is concerned with such a matter as dangerous illness. It has been suggested that the connection is to be found in the belief that sickness and many other calamities were due to the action of evil spirits, either acting, as it were, on their own account, or let loose on the victim by some human enemy possessed of magical powers. This hypothesis does at least something to mitigate the vindictive spirit for which so many of our Psalms have been justly criticized as, for example, in the case of Ps. 109. Another good illustration is to be seen in Ps. 7. The Psalmist is conscious of complete innocence ; he has done wrong to no man, least of all to the man who has brought him into mortal danger. The Psalmist prays first for his own deliverance, but that is not enough, and the latter part of the Psalm is occupied with a prayer that vengeance may fall on the adversary. But this is not mere passion for revenge. The enemy has set loose an evil force of some kind, and it is bound, sooner or later, to claim a victim. Since that is so, it would seem only right that the sufferer should be the man who has launched the deadly thing on the world, for no reason except to gratify his own malice and spite. It would be manifestly unfair for any other, especially for the innocent person against whom it was directed, to have to bear the weight of calamity which this thing will inevitably bring in its train.

It must never be forgotten that the ancient Hebrew, like others of his time, lived in the midst of a world which was peopled by personal beings, often invisible, yet capable of doing good or evil to man. Animistic ideas are slow to die, even in the presence of a higher faith, and the whole history of man's religious life attests the enduring power of belief in demons. From time to time we meet with expressions and even passages in the Psalter which can best be explained by reference to this type of thought. Thus in Ps. 91 : 5f. we have a list of the perils from which the faithful will be delivered. They include "the pestilence that walketh in darkness"—clearly conceived as a personal being, while the "destruction" of the latter part of v. 6 is almost certainly to be understood as the name of a demon "Qeteb."

It is, however, fairly clear that all the enemies from whom Psalmists pray to be delivered are not necessarily sorcerers and evil spirits. In some instances we have words which are derived from legal process, and though this may sometimes—indeed often—be simply a metaphor, there is surely some ground for supposing that we have in certain instances forms of prayer which might be used by a litigant protesting his innocence. It must be remembered that in ancient Israel, and elsewhere in the East, evidence had to be very convincing to be accepted. Normally it had to be offered by an eye-witness—probably by more than one—and circumstantial evidence had to be very clear. In the absence of any direct indication of the truth or falsehood of a charge, the suit might be terminated by one or other of the parties (in a civil dispute) or the accused (in a criminal case) taking an oath. In the Aramaic papyri found at Elephantine we have examples of oaths taken in support of claims to property, and the record of the oath is part of the owner's title, and must be handed on with other deeds when the property is transferred to another owner. The idea of legal process was never very far from the Israelite mind ; the poem of Job, for instance, is unintelligible unless we recognize that the writer contemplates a great trial scene in which the sufferer is to hear the charges which God will bring against him, and the discussion concludes in ch. 31 with a great oath of purgation. Another method was, clearly, to bring the matter to the sanctuary and secure a verdict from Yahweh, given, of course, through the priests. It is not improbable that they made use of the sacred lot in ascertaining the divine verdict on a difficult case, and it is natural, indeed, almost inevitable, that the ceremony which accompanied the casting of the lot should include an appeal and a protestation of innocence by the accused. We may take Ps. 26 as an example. The speaker begins " Judge me, O Yahweh, for I have walked in my perfection "—using a word which implies that he is nowhere open to a criminal charge. He is ready, even anxious, to have Yahweh testing him, for he knows that the most searching examination will reveal nothing in him that ought not to be there. He protests that he has had no dealings with false men, and that he hates the company of evildoers. He has washed his hands in innocence—a metaphor for the upright life which we meet again in Ps. 73 : 13, where it looks like a recognized formula—and his only delight has been in the worship of Yahweh. He pleads that he may not be classed with offenders, and ends much as he began. We may well believe that he pauses at the end of his statement and waits for the result of his appeal. It is favourable, and the last verse reads like the response of a man who has been set free from suspicion. In other cases we have less assertion of innocence, and more of the appeal for deliverance. An illustration of this tendency may be found in Ps. 142, whose author—or speaker—was, to judge from v. 7, actually in prison.

It is natural to turn from the laments of the individual to the thanksgiving of the individual. We may assume that this type of Psalm originated, like others, in the cultus, and if that is so, then the particular occasion was almost certainly that of the Thank-offering. Sometimes we can follow the actual procedure. In Ps. 66, for example, the Psalmist says (v. 13) that he is entering the house of Yahweh to perform his vows. He is bringing with him sacrificial animals for the burnt-offering, and summons all hearers to witness his act and its meaning. He tells them all that he has appealed to Yahweh for help, and adds that Yahweh would not have heard him if his heart had not been free from evil. Then we must suppose a gap in the text, which would be filled in on every separate occasion with a recital of the particular circumstances in which the vow had been made. Finally he repeats his statement that Yahweh has heard him and granted his request, and adds an expression of gratitude.

Another good example is to be seen in Ps. 116. This is a form which might be used by a person who had suffered from some terrible sickness. Apparently, too, it had involved him in suspicion of some crime, for he seems to have had human adversaries. It may, however, be suggested that the Psalm was intended to cover more than one type of suppliant, and that the Psalmist inserted verses which might be omitted if the circumstances did not apply. Here, as in most of these Psalms, the writer begins with an ascription of praise, though the text may be in some disorder. Then follows the reason : Yahweh has delivered him from deadly peril in answer to his appeal. The danger in v. 3 seems to have been due to disease, but other references, e.g., to his own humble condition (v. 6) and to the falsity of men (v. 11) are adapted rather to some legal matter—a criminal charge or a civil action. Then in v. 12 he puts the ritual question " what shall I render unto Yahweh . . . ?" and gives the answer, presumably dictated by the priest in attendance, " I will take the cup of salvation and call upon the name of Yahweh." Clearly we have here a piece of ritual, with which we may compare the meal to which allusion is made in Ps. 22 : 26. The ceremonial continues as the worshipper actually offers the substance of his vow and slays the sacrificial animal (v. 17), and so brings this part of the proceedings to an end.

Other details are suggested by different Psalms, though we must not forget that they were not all necessarily present in every performance of the thanksgiving rite. From time to time an appeal is made to others to share in the recognition of Yahweh's goodness ; the most comprehensive example is to be seen in Ps. 66, where the whole earth is summoned to break into a cry of greeting to God. In Ps. 118 we have three classes of people enumerated—Israel, the house of Aaron, and those who fear Yahweh ; all are bidden praise Yahweh " for His love is for ever." Elsewhere we get the impression that there are other worshippers present on the occasion. Ps. 34 : 3, for example, calls on the whole company : " Magnify Yahweh with me ; let us exalt His name together." Ps. 116 : 14 simply assumes that there is a gathering of people in the sanctuary while the offering is being made ; in this case, however, they are not asked to participate except as witnesses to the fact that the vow has been fulfilled. Evidently different forms of ceremonial might be employed on various occasions, perhaps depending on the nature of the vow in respect of which the offering was made, perhaps on the time and date at which it was presented.

Like some other classes, these hymns of private thanksgiving often had an introductory formula, which might be more or less extended. Pss. 30, 34, 116, 138 all begin with an expression of the singer's feeling of gratitude and affection to Yahweh, while Ps. 92 announces in more general and sober terms that it is a good thing to give thanks (or praise) to Yahweh. In this case we have an introduction extending to three verses, followed by a transitional passage (vv. 4-8) in which praise is mingled with a general statement of benefits received. Then comes the more detailed reason for gratitude ; the enemies of God (who are identical with the enemies of the Psalmist) have perished, while the righteous (in this instance clearly represented by the Psalmist himself) flourish as luxuriant trees to a green old age.

In addition to the classes which have been mentioned, Gunkel enumerates others which he calls " smaller," though some of them include a fairly numerous group. First among these we may notice those which may come under the general head of blessings and curses. It may be as well to recall the fact that in the earlier stages of intellectual development the spoken word might be, and often was, regarded as being in itself efficient. Its power depended partly on the personality of the speaker who uttered it, but there were occasions in the life of most people when they became " fey," and what they said might control future events. A man or woman at the point of death, for example, would deliver sentences which were not merely predictions due to fore-knowledge, but in themselves the active agents which brought about the result indicated. No small part of the influence of the prophet lay in the belief that his oracle " would not return void, but would accomplish that whereunto it was sent." Now the expert, that is the magician or other especially endowed person, would best achieve his purpose by putting his sentences into some sort of artificial form, and we have sometimes suggestions which lead us to suspect that this was the original purpose of some types of poetry. When, for instance, Deborah is exhorted to " utter a song," it certainly looks as if this "song" were to be some inspired utterance which would secure the rout of the enemy, and this view is strengthened by the fact that she is first bidden "awake," which may well imply the rousing of the magical prophetic personality (Jud. 5 : 12). Of course, by the time we reach the literary period of Israel's history, this feeling had largely disappeared (though traces of it are almost ineradicable).

The forms, however, remained, and in a fair number of Psalms we have phrases which take us back to the old view. Several of our Psalms begin with words rendered in EVV as "blessed," and others have the expression later on. Ps. 1 begins "Blessed is the man . . ." Other examples are Pss. 32, 41, 112, 128. The term used in these cases is almost an interjection—"O the blessing of . . . !", and what follows in the Psalm is descriptive of the happiness of the person concerned. The righteous devotee of the Law, for example, will be like a tree planted by rivers of water. An example of the blessing occurring in the middle of a Psalm may be seen in Ps. 84 : 4, 5, where it is called down, first on those who dwell in the house of Yahweh and then on the man whose strength is in Yahweh.

On the other side we have frequent reference to the calamities and the misery which will be the lot of the wicked. Often we find that the Psalmist is calling for disaster on his adversaries. Though the actual word "cursed" does not occur in this formal way in the Psalter, we do find it in Jer. 17 : 5-8, a passage which, apparently, formed the model for Ps. 1, and we may assume that language like that of the latter part of this Psalm may well have had the effect of a formal curse. As we have already noted, such curses are often, perhaps normally, attempts to turn back on the enemy a force which he has let loose against the Psalmist. The words have been uttered, the stroke must fall somewhere, let it come back in boomerang fashion on the head of the man from whom it originally proceeded. A recognition of this fact goes some way to minimise the sense of vindictiveness which so often troubles readers of the Psalter ; the motive behind these expressions is not so much hatred or a desire for vengeance as a wish to escape a weapon which has already been launched. At the same time we are forced to admit that this explanation will not fit all the examples ; the closing words of Ps. 137, for instance, are simply a demand for retribution which we may understand but cannot approve. Both blessings and curses are frequently found in Psalms which may also come under some other category.

This last point may be well illustrated by reference to a Psalm which has already been cited as an example of a "Blessing"—Ps. 128. It is one of the group designated in the A.V. as "Songs of Degrees," and in the R.V. as "Songs of Ascents," which may well be taken to imply songs of pilgrimage, to be used by worshippers on their way up to the sanctuary at Jerusalem from some distant home. True, Gunkel himself assigns only one of these pieces to that special function. This is Ps. 122, and he adds to it Ps. 84. We may, however, include also Ps. 15 and Ps. 24 : 3-6, which state the qualifications required of the worshipper. Moreover in the " official " group of " Songs of Ascents," we frequently meet with expressions which would well suit a traveller on a sacred journey as he draws near to his goal. Thus he " lifts up his eyes unto the hills " (Ps. 121 : 1) as he crosses the coastal plain from the west. When he reaches the heights he will have seen Jerusalem compassed about with mountains (Ps. 125 : 2). Ps. 132 expresses the determination of the worshipper to reach his goal, and his intense devotion to the holy city. The series concludes with an appeal to the worshippers, who are exhorted to acts of adoration, such as would be appropriate to pilgrims when they find themselves on the actual threshhold of the Temple.

" Songs of Victory " form a class of which we have already seen examples among the poems now preserved in the historical books of the Old Testament. But this element appears in the thought of several poems, e.g., in Ps. 46 we have a picture of Yahweh putting an end to all war by the complete overthrow of the hostile armies and the destruction of their weapons. Ps. 76 comes as near as any to giving a complete example of this kind of paean. Here we notice that it is Yahweh and Yahweh alone who achieves the victory, and He works in miraculous fashion. He has only to utter a rebuke, and the enemy sinks down in slumber, and the poet uses a word which suggests the deep sleep which only God can induce for His special purposes, such a sleep as fell on Adam that a rib might be taken from him, or on Abram when the covenant-making God appeared to him. But while the subject is not infrequent, formal Psalms of this type have not been preserved in the Psalter, and we are led to suspect that, in the age of compilation, Israel had no specific service of thanksgiving for victory. Probably forms used in other kinds of thanksgiving could be employed when necessary.

Two or three of our Psalms, notably Pss. 78, 105 and 106 have a certain historical character. They tell the story of Yahweh's dealings with His people, and seem to be fairly late in construction, since they presuppose the completed narratives of the Hexateuch. They have contacts with the " Hymns " for, naturally, the people are summoned to praise Yahweh for His marvellous acts.

As might be expected, these narratives have a didactic purpose ; Ps. 106 in particular is an attempt to warn Israel against a further repetition of their frequent failures and apostasies of ancient days. Here the story is carried down to the occupation of Palestine, and while it ostensibly does not go beyond the period of the Judges, it is obviously coloured by the experiences and events of the monarchy, perhaps even of the exile.

Of " Law-Psalms," Gunkel recognizes only elements in Ps. 50. It must be remembered that the Hebrew " Torah " does not mean merely " Law " in our sense of the word, but rather a piece of divine instruction, and Gunkel's point here is that it is only in this Psalm that fresh instructions as to worship are given. Curiously enough, these are hardly in general accord with the tendency of the formal " Law," since the insistence is not on the familiar forms of sacrifice, but on a deeper, more spiritual devotion to the moral will of Yahweh.

It is, perhaps, hardly correct to speak of " prophetic Psalms " ; what is meant is a prophetic, or rather an eschatological element which appears in a number of Psalms which really belong to different types. Thus we have this kind of thought in hymns of praise like Ps. 98, while the songs of the divine enthronement may naturally develop an apocalyptic flavour, as in Pss. 47, 93, 97 and others. Ps. 50, at which we have just looked, begins with a theophany of the true eschatological type. The fact that in this, and possibly in other Psalms as well, the eschatological element could be removed without impairing other features of the message, suggests that possibly the apocalpytic factor is a later addition to, or modification of, the original form. There were periods in Israelite history, particularly times of depression and distress, when men's minds naturally turned to the hope of a catastrophic divine intervention and the overthrow of the existing world order. It is to be expected that we should find traces of this feeling in many forms of Jewish worship, and where this was not obvious it might well, in certain cases, be made explicit.

A more strictly prophetic outlook is to be seen in one or two Psalms which emphasize the futility of the cultus. This is rather surprising in a collection whose primary object was evidently to serve the purposes of worship, and it attests the strength of the feeling handed down from great teachers of spiritual religion like the eighth and seventh century prophets. But we cannot deny the presence of this element in Psalms like 50 and 51, though it is interesting to note that in the form preserved in our Bibles an attempt is usually made to correct the anti-sacrificial feeling by the addition of a sentence or two justifying, or even enjoining, that type of religion which the poet elsewhere deprecates.

Just as some Psalms contain prophetic or apocalyptic elements, so others suggest the influence of the " wisdom " type of thought. This manifests itself mainly in two directions. One is the appearance of short pithy summaries of experience—what we commonly call " proverbs," and the other is to be seen in the discussion of some deeper problem of religion or ethics. A good example of the last type is to be found in Ps. 49, which deals with the age-long question of the suffering of the righteous and the success of the wicked. The conclusion reached by the writer is that in reality the wealth accumulated by injustice is of no real value, since the owner can take nothing with him when he dies. A similar theme dominates other Psalms, especially Pss. 37 and 73, though the two reach very different conclusions. To the other type belong a number of passages in the

Psalter. Ps. 78 opens very much like some of the chapters in the Book of Proverbs, and actually uses the word "Mashal," which is the ordinary term for "proverb." The remainder of the Psalm, however, is a poetic summary of Israel's history down to the establishment of the monarchy, described in order to illustrate the dangers of forgetting the "instruction" which people like the Psalmist could give. At other times we have the distinction between the wise man and the fool, so characteristic of this thought-area, as in Ps. 94 : 8. In Ps. 34 : 12ff we have a string of sentences which recall the form common in Proverbs. Verses like Ps. 37 : 16 are of the same type ; indeed the alphabetic Psalm lends itself to this kind of thought.

As we glance over these various types, together with Psalms in which we have two or more types interchanging, we realize that we must not draw lines of demarcation too hard and fast. But such a classification as that which Gunkel has given us does open the way for a new approach to the study of the Psalter. To a certain extent it helps us to place a particular piece, especially where a whole poem is clearly designed for use in some form of ritual. One result is that to-day we ascribe to the pre-exilic age a far larger element in the Psalter than would have been done by leading scholars fifty years ago. The study of the pre-exilic cultus is in its infancy, and much is still to be learnt from comparison with the practices of other religions. Chief among these will doubtless be the forms of worship which were current in the ancient Ugaritian community whose remains have recently been unearthed at Ras Shamra. The sacred texts already deciphered shew a sacrificial and liturgical system not unlike that of the Old Testament, and the presumption is that a similar type of ritual was observed at the Israelite sanctuaries during the period of the monarchy. It is, however, too early yet to speak of assured conclusions, and we must, for the time, be content with a general expectation of fuller knowledge.

VIII

THE PSALMS : III

IT goes without saying that Israel was not the only people in the ancient east who possessed a rich store of religious poetry. In particular a number of pieces have come down to us from the two great centres of civilization, those of Mesopotamia and of the Nile. In many ways both exercised considerable influence on the thought of Palestine, though in different directions. Generally speaking, it was in ages preceding the advent of the Aramaean invaders after the Exodus that Babylonian influence was most directly exercised, and for the most part this seems to have reached Israel through the Canaanites whom they found in Palestine. The most obvious instance is that of law, for the earliest Israelite codes and the well-known Babylonian and Assyrian codes clearly have a common basis. There is, however, no question of direct borrowing, for, strangely enough, of all the forms this type of law took, the Israelite is the most primitive. The facts can hardly be explained except on the supposition that its basis had been long known, centuries indeed before the age of Hammurabi, in Palestine, and that there it had remained more or less stationary, while in the land of its origin it had steadily developed to meet the growing needs of a progressive community.

Now we find in Babylonian sacred literature numbers of Psalms which in many respects recall those of the Hebrew Psalter. The best known are probably the so-called " Penitential Psalms," in which the soul of the worshipper is poured out in confession and a longing for forgiveness. It is not unnatural that we should detect similarities of expression in the hymns of the two countries, since the minds of each people would tend to move in much the same direction, and the human need in the face of sin and its punishment is alike all the world over. We do, as a matter of fact, not infrequently note the appearance of similar thoughts, metaphors and even actual phrases in both literatures. The resemblances, however, are not so close or so numerous as to compel us to think of direct borrowing, and many of the best judges would agree that they are to be ascribed partly to identity of conditions and partly to the common heritage of the Semitic mind.

The case is rather different when we turn to Egypt. The empire of the Nile had occupied Palestine immediately before the arrival of Israel, and was always close at hand. What is surprising is to find, not that Egypt exercised so much influence on the religion of Israel, but that she exercised so little. So far as we can reconstruct the Hebrew cultus and the mythology with which it was connected, it belongs emphatically to the general type represented by Mesopotamia and northern Syria rather than to that current in Egypt. But we do find certain literary similarities which shew acquaintance, and perhaps more than mere acquaintance, with the sacred writings of Egypt. This is particularly evident when we look at some of the literature which belongs roughly to the fifteenth and fourteenth centuries B.C. This was a period when Israel was still in process of formation ; the date of the Exodus is much disputed, but it would be generally agreed, even by those who place it as early as possible, that there was no organized Israelite state in the middle of the fourteenth century. That is the age in which we find one of the most striking religious movements of ancient times, the reforms of Ikhnaton (Amenhotep IV). This is no place to discuss these in detail ; it must be enough to note that the new theology seems to have been definitely monotheistic, or at least to have exalted the Sun-god to the exclusion of all other cults. In the proverbial literature of that age—including collections which come one or two centuries before and after the reign of Ikhnaton—we find a stress on ethics which strongly recalls the attitude of the best Israelite minds as represented in the Prophets and some of the Psalms. When we turn from didactic to more strictly religious literature, we are even more impressed by similarity in thought and even in language. Expressions of repentance for sin and requests for pardon will tend everywhere to take the same general form, but this does not explain the close resemblance in actual words which we sometimes meet in reading Egyptian and Hebrew penitential hymns alongside of one another. The best-known illustration of resemblance, however, is in a hymn of praise. We possess a hymn to the Sun-god, composed by Ikhnaton, which is very like Ps. 104, and it is generally agreed that the two cannot be independent. We read lines like these :

> When thou goest down in the western horizon,
> The earth is in darkness as if it were dead . . .
> Every lion cometh forth from his den,
> And all snakes that bite . . .

or

> The ships voyage up and down the stream likewise,
> Every way is open because thou risest.
> The fishes in the river leap before thy face ;
> Thy rays are in the great green sea. . . . ..

or again

The earth is in thy hand,
For thou hast made them.
When thou arisest they live,
When thou settest they die.

Such passages irresistibly remind us of the language of
the Psalm :

He appointeth the moon for seasons :
The sun knoweth his going down.
Thou makest darkness, and it is night ;
Wherein all the beasts of the forest do creep forth.
The young lions roar after their prey,
And seek their meat from God.

*   *   *

Yonder is the sea, great and wide,
Wherein are things creeping innumerable,
Both small and great beasts.
There go the ships ;
There is that Leviathan whom thou hast formed to take
        his pastime therein.

*   *   *

Thou openest thine hand, they are satisfied with good.
Thou hidest thy face, they are troubled ;
And takest away their breath, they die
And return to their dust.

Here it seems to be beyond dispute that the Hebrew
poet was at least acquainted with the Egyptian hymn,
and we are, then, justified in suspecting that elsewhere,
even if the resemblance is less exact, there was in Palestine
a certain measure of familiarity with other Egyptian
sacred poems.

When we consider these facts, it becomes the more
remarkable that there were wide differences in thought
between the Hebrew and the Egyptian Psalmists. The
whole thought of Egypt, for example, was oriented to a
doctrine of a life after death ; a belief in immortality,
even in resurrection, goes back to a comparatively early

date, and may be as old as the pyramids. But nowhere in the Old Testament Psalter have we a clear statement of such a doctrine. Several passages have been interpreted in that sense, but nowhere is it the only possible interpretation, and where we are considering a new or unfamiliar position, we can be satisfied with nothing less than absolute certainty ; no reasonable alternative explanation must be rejected. The clearest case is probably Ps. 73 : 26. Even this is disputed, and it is justly remarked that the Hebrew rendered " for ever " may mean a long time, but is by no means necessarily eternity in our sense of the word. At the same time the poet does speak of his flesh and his heart coming to an end, ceasing to exist, and his communion with God is contrasted with this perishing of his physical frame. It would appear, then, that we may fairly interpret the passage as implying that death is not the end of relations between God and man. This is neither a full doctrine of immortality nor a statement of resurrection, but when once man's thought has overcome the barrier of death these things may in time follow.

Even if this view of Ps. 73 : 26 be right, it remains an isolated passage. Much more normal is the kind of expression we find in Ps. 6 : 5 :

> There is no remembrance of thee in death ;
> In She'ol who shall praise thee ?

In Ps. 88 : 10-12, again, we have :

> Wilt thou do thy marvel for the dead ?
> Or shall the shades rise and praise thee ?
> Shall the tale of thy love be told in the grave ?
> Thy faithfulness in Abaddon ?
> Can thy wonder be known in the darkness ?
> Thy righteousness in the land of oblivion ?

Less keenly emotional, but just as clear is Ps. 115 : 17 :

The dead praise not Yah,
   Nor they that go down into silence.

But if on this point Egyptian thinking was centuries ahead of that which we find in Israel, in other ways it was the Hebrew who made the greatest advances. In spite of the efforts made by Ikhnaton to establish a form of theology which at least approximates to monotheism, the general trend of Egyptian religion was polytheistic, with a strong undercurrent of animism. In fact its average level declined instead of rising with the passing of the centuries. In Israel, on the other hand, the old traditions inherited from the Mosaic age insisted on the worship of a single deity, and though this ideal was seldom realized in practice during the monarchy, there were always groups which stood for the cult of Yahweh and Yahweh alone as the national God, while He was universally recognized as the supreme object of worship for Israel. Even as late as the fifth century we find in the strange Jewish community at Elephantine more than one deity mentioned, but the personal names which have come down to us are compounded with no other divine element than that of Yahweh. It is in harmony with this development, which led in the end to a pure monotheism, that we find in many of our Psalms traces, and more than traces, of polytheistic beliefs. The phenomenon is most striking in cases where Yahweh is exalted at the expense of other gods. It is sometimes rather disguised in the ordinary English versions. E.g., Ps. 29 opens :

   Give unto Yahweh, ye sons of gods (Elim),
     Give unto Yahweh glory and strength.

Again in Ps. 96 : 5 the phrase " all the gods of the nations are idols " should not be held to imply that foreign deities are merely objects of wood, stone or metal. The word rendered " idols " is simply a contemptuous diminutive, and is not to be taken as denying their actual personal existence. Ps. 97 : 7 is worth noting in this connection : " Let them be ashamed, all that serve a graven image, which boast ' idols ' ; bow before him all ye gods." Here the direct address to the gods shews that the " idols ", even the " graven image ", either are or represent real personal beings, though they are inferior to Yahweh. It is in the Psalms of Yahweh's enthronement that we find most of these expressions. Thus in Ps. 95 : 3 " For Yahweh is a great God (El), and a great king above all gods." Parallel expressions occur in Pss. 96 : 4, 97 : 9. But the idea appears elsewhere, e.g., in Ps. 86 : 8 : " There is none like unto thee among the gods, O Lord, nor any works like thine." cf. also Ps. 89 : 6. As we have already noticed, in all these instances the other gods are mentioned in order to emphasize the pre-eminence of Yahweh. Sometimes we get a picture of a heavenly court, consisting of divine beings whose president and king is Yahweh. Thus in Ps. 138 : 1 the poet finds himself in the presence of the gods, and makes his confession of praise not only before men but also before the divine assembly. More striking still is Ps. 82, where it seems that Yahweh, as supreme ruler of the universe, summons before him all the other gods. They have been entrusted with the government of parts of the world, and they have failed so badly that they are to be degraded to the level of ordinary human beings and to become subject to the same law of mortality as are men. This may indicate a transition from the acceptance of the full godhead of these other " gods " to a doctrine which left them superhuman but definitely relegated them to a second order of being. Even if Yahweh is the supreme ruler of the universe, He may yet employ subordinate agents to carry out His wishes in detail. A similar idea appears in the commonly accepted doctrine of angels—beings who are surely superfluous in the service of an omnipotent Personality, who can accomplish His will by the simplest flash of thought. Indeed, while a belief in angels (This, of course, has no reference to the Old Testament conception of the " Angel of Yahweh," who is essentially a form or manifestation of Yahweh Himself) doubtless owes much to Persian influence, especially in distinguishing between good angels and evil, it may well be found, on careful examination, that the way had long been prepared by the subordinate status assigned to other gods.

Even if the Psalter as a whole does not present us with a pure monotheism, there is no doubt as to the absolute supremacy of Yahweh. Many times we find reference to His work in creation. The heavens are the work of His fingers (Ps. 8 : 3), the sea is His and He made it, and His hands formed the dry land (Ps. 95 : 5). Instances are too numerous to mention ; nearly every hymn of praise contains some reference to the work of Yahweh in creation. Occasionally we meet with language which suggests a popular mythology akin to that of Mesopotamia. In Ps. 89 : 10, 11, for example, we have :

> Thou hast broken Rahab in pieces as one that is slain,
> Thou hast scattered thine enemies with the arm of thy strength,
> The heavens are thine, the earth also is thine,
> The world and the fulness thereof, thou hast founded them.

The last line shews that the poet is thinking of creation, and we at once recall the story of the rebellious Chaos-monster, here called Rahab, who, with her associates, was destroyed by the hero-god, the universe then being formed from her sundered body. Again in Ps. 74 : 13, 14 we read :

Thou didst divide the sea by thy strength ;
    Thou breakest the heads of the dragons in the waters.
Thou breakest the heads of Leviathan in pieces,
    Thou gavest him to be meat to the people inhabiting
        the wilderness.

The whole passage, vv. 12-17 is an appeal to the power manifested in creation, and we think inevitably of the old story again, though the name of the monster this time is Leviathan—a term which seems to be used in the same sense in Is. 27 : 1. Ugaritic mythology, too, presents us with a seven-headed monster. With its polytheistic background the myth has been carefully excluded from the official religious documents of Israel, but it almost certainly existed, and a few casual expressions are best explained as referring to it. They were probably overlooked because they would suggest the myth only to those who were familiar with it.

In numerous passages, too, Yahweh's control of all natural phenomena is stressed. Again, instances are too numerous to give in detail, but we may note that occasionally a whole Psalm is devoted to some such theme as this ; Ps. 104 is an excellent example. But in many other pieces there are allusions to Yahweh's power as exhibited in nature. Volcanic action, which could have been known only by hearsay to the untravelled Israelite, is suggested by a phrase like " touch the hills and they will smoke " (Ps. 144 : 5). An earthquake may be due to the presence of Yahweh " The earth shook and trembled, the foundations also of the mountains moved, and were shaken because he was wroth " (Ps. 18 : 7). The regular processes of the physical world, too, were not forgotten, though the eastern mind more readily sees God in the abnormal than in the normal. Ps. 104, again, is an admirable illustration, while Ps. 107 gives a whole series of circumstances in which His power over nature is exercised for the good of those who cry to Him.

It is not only in Nature that Yahweh's supremacy is manifested ; it appears also in history. The Psalmists seldom, if ever, go so far as some of the prophets do, and ascribe the government of foreign nations to Yahweh, whether they affect Israel directly or not. But they frequently dwell on the story of their own people, and references to the Exodus are particularly common. In passing we may note how seldom the name of Moses appears, especially in earlier Psalms. But there is no doubt that the deliverance from Egypt was the historical event which, more than any other, dominated the thinking of the Psalmists, and, indeed, of all Israelites. Sometimes we have regular poetical summaries of history, as in Pss. 78, 105 and 106. Ps. 136 combines the celebration of Yahweh as creator with thanks to Him as the controller of Israel's fortunes. Sometimes the worshipper in private or national distress appeals to the great stories of the past and asks that they may be repeated. Thus we get casual references in such passages as Pss. 80 : 8-11, 81 : 5, 10, 114 : 1 ff., 135 : 8 ff. and many other places.

All these celebrate the great goodness and favour shown to Israel by Yahweh. But the greatest of His gifts was the Law, and more than once we have fairly extensive passages in recognition of the fact. The latter part of Ps. 19 is devoted to the subject, and the longest of all the Psalms, the alphabetic acrostic of Ps. 119, is a somewhat artificial expansion of the same theme. There are slighter allusions to it, e.g., in Ps. 103 : 7.

The common appeal to Yahweh by the oppressed, whether the nation or the individual, is based on two presuppositions. One is that Yahweh has all power, and the other is that He is absolutely just. As we have seen, such application to Him is often reinforced by recollection of the great things He has done in the past. God can see His own people saved and restored, if only He will. And with one consent the Psalmists are certain that if He is only convinced of the justice of their case, He will see that they get their due. Indeed, they could hardly have entered the court unless they had felt satisfied that they were in the right. Litigation is one of the commonest features of oriental life, and, as far as we can see, it has been so from the dawn of civilisation. The forensic metaphor, then, is very frequent, and, indeed, the whole conception of righteousness has the flavour of the law. The "righteous" person is he who wins his case, and we have already seen the part played by the idea in the Book of Job. Consequently we often meet with legal phraseology even when Israel's plea is for deliverance from national enemies. Ps. 43, for example, begins with an appeal that Yahweh will "judge" the unhappy exile and "plead his cause," though here there is no question of a human court of law. As we have already seen, however, a certain number of the Psalms may have been composed definitely for the use of plaintiff or defendant. Some are or contain protestations of innocence, though the greatest of these lies outside the Psalter and is to be found in Job 31. It is quite possible that these were formulae used in taking an oath. It is clear that if one or other of the parties could be induced to swear to the justice of his case, that settled the matter. It is interesting to note that the offence of perjury was practically unthinkable ; no man would expose himself to the vengeance of a god whose name had been taken " in vain," i.e., to a falsehood.

As a rule statements of innocence are confined to, or adapted to, particular occasions, and give us no list of the righteous acts to be performed or the sins to be avoided by the worshippers of Yahweh. It may be assumed, however, that He Himself is held to be perfectly good, as far as men understood goodness. This does not mean that their standards were always such as we could accept to-day. In particular we have not infrequent calls for divine punishment on those who have done wrong to the petitioner. Our own feeling revolts against such a prayer as that with which Ps. 137 ends. The Psalm itself is a beautiful lament over the sufferings of Israel in exile and the cruelties which have been perpetrated by the conqueror, but it concludes " Blessed be he that shall seize thy babes and dash them upon the rock." To us who have been taught to forgive our enemies this is a direct violation of moral principle—but how human it is ! If we had seen and borne what the Psalmist saw and endured, we might well have endorsed his curse. Centuries must elapse before the true principle was stated, and we may doubt whether it has even yet been fully learned.

At the same time we are forced to recognize the fact that the emphasis is always laid on conduct rather than on ritual. It is true that there are frequent references to the ceremonial of Israel, and the highest hopes and desires of the worshipper usually centre round the Temple cult. It could hardly be otherwise in a corpus of poetry mainly designed for use in worship of one kind or another. Evidence of this feeling may be seen in such utterances as Ps. 42-3, or in the very familiar Ps. 100—to mention only a couple out of innumerable instances. Even in those rare instances where the Psalmist adopts a prophetic attitude to sacrifice, as in Ps. 51, the editors felt it necessary to correct any misapprehension by appending a note of their own, stressing the importance of the ritual. But when the penitent came to confess his wrong-doing before God, it was seldom, if ever, that his sin consisted in an offence against the ceremonial law. Here we have a striking contrast to what we find so often in non-Israelite Psalms and in those votive tablets which the archaeologist discovers in the ruined shrines of other nations. What has aroused the anger of Yahweh, what has brought the worshipper into peril, is nearly always a breach of the moral law. In full harmony with this position, when we find a statement of the qualifications demanded of Yahweh's worshippers, as we do in passages like Pss. 15 and 24 : 3-6, the list is entirely composed of ethical items. We never hear the suppliant admit to failure in the matter of sacrifices, nor is it required of him that all his levitical obligations have been fulfilled before he can enter the presence of his God.

We are, then, the more impressed by the overwhelming sense of sin in the mind of the Psalmists. True, many of the pieces in the book are prayers for deliverance from suffering or danger which is assumed to be a punishment for sin, but there can be no doubt as to the sincerity of the confessions which we read. It is significant in itself that when the Israelite met with disaster he was at once reminded of his own evil ways. This, of course, is not invariably the point of view adopted by the worshipper, and sometimes the poet is simply bewildered by an appearance of punishment when he is unconscious of sin. As we have seen, such protestations of innocence are natural where the speaker is in court, rebutting a charge of crime brought against him by his enemies. But in numerous other cases we have the simple acknowledgment of faults. " Behold I was shapen in iniquity, and in sin did my mother conceive me " (Ps. 51 : 5) is not meant to be a statement of " original sin," still less a slur on the mother's character ; it is merely the poet's way of expressing his own intense feeling of sinfulness in the presence of an utterly pure and holy God. It is particularly notice-able that no wrong is ever done to man alone. True, it is the sinner's neighbour who is the immediate sufferer, but the wrong done to him fades into insignificance as compared with the yet deeper injury inflicted on God. "Against thee, thee only, have I sinned" (Ps. 51 : 4) is the genuine cry of a heart which realises the truth that God is the greatest sufferer in the universe. Taken as a whole this Psalm has no exact parallel elsewhere in the book, but that is in no small measure because it sums up and makes explicit much that lies beneath the surface of other pieces.

What then is God's attitude towards sin ? Condemna-tion and punishment—these are the first and most obvious signs of His reaction to it. A people who held so strongly to a doctrine of an absolutely righteous God could hardly have taken any other view. But that is not all. His justice is tempered, and more than tempered, with mercy, a mercy which springs out of and is controlled by love. We may look at a poem like Ps. 103 ; it is an expression of much that we find elsewhere in the Psalter. It is a hymn of the divine love, that love which shews itself in so many different forms. That which is most stressed here is the love of a person who is in some way bound to another, and has certain obligations laid on him by that relationship. It is what our versions feebly represent by the term "mercy" in vv. 11, 17 and often elsewhere in the Bible. It implies that God has in some way sub-jected Himself to conditions of His own making. He is the creator of all mankind, therefore He has responsi-bilities towards us :

> "Thou wilt not leave us in the dust ;
> Thou madest man. . . ."

is the English poet's way of expressing the thought. We need not dwell here on the various ways in which the Psalmist sees this love made manifest. But there is another aspect which is stressed here. It springs out of the human consciousness of insignificance in the divine presence, the reaction of the infinitesimal to the infinite. There is a great gulf between the ephemeral and the eternal. God is as much aware of this as we are :

> " He knoweth our frame,
> He remembereth that we are dust."

God realizes the way in which His creatures are constructed ; He understands their constitution, with all its weakness as well as its possibilities. And so His attitude is more than that of a creator ; it is that of a father. Disguised by the English " pity " we have another aspect of love. This is the ideal attitude of the parent to the child. Etymologically mother-love, it has become that of the father as well, and has lost nothing of its tenderness in the transfer. Such love cannot be satisfied with mere justice, and, indeed, it may be questioned whether mere justice is ever real justice at all. And so we find that the experience of the Psalmist is essentially one of forgiveness. That is how he begins when he thinks of the various manifestations of Yahweh's love. " Who forgiveth all thine iniquities " comes even before " Who healeth all thy diseases." The way is prepared for the great sentences of v. 8 ff. :

> " Parentally tender and freely loving is Yahweh ;
>> Slow to anger, and great in love,
> He will not always argue against us,
>> Nor will he keep His anger for ever.
>
> Not as our sins have deserved has he dealt with us,
>> Nor as our iniquities have merited has he requited us.
> For as heaven is high above the earth,

So high is His love to those who fear Him.
As far as the east is from the west,
   So far has he removed our deliberate transgressions
      from us."

It is true that Christian thought cannot fail to observe a certain limitation in all this. The love of Yahweh, great as it is (and the Psalmist uses the largest units of measurement possible to him), operates only on those who are already in the right attitude—" them that fear Him." But we must not ask for too much. It is true that in the Old Testament there are adumbrations of the truth that God takes the initiative in the elimination of sin and its effects, but these are comparatively rare, and are far above the ordinary level of Hebrew religious thought. We must not look for the parable of the lost sheep even in the Psalter.

But to the Psalm again which we have already touched. The natural affection of the parent for the child is the attitude of the great person for the small, the eternal for the evanescent. In the absence of a full doctrine of life after death, in which the relation between the worshipper and his God would be maintained, it was inevitable that men should dwell on the contrast between the endless life of God and the little span of human existence. This is far from being the only passage in which this rises to the surface ; Ps. 90, for example, is essentially a cry for something that will endure after all that makes personality in man has ceased to be. But Ps. 103 does not stop with this thought ; Yahweh's reaction to his ephemeral children is one of tender consideration :

   " He knows all about our structure,
      He remembers that we are dust."

At once, however, the Psalmist comes back to his main theme, and he recognises the eternity of God's love, showered generation after generation on the faithful :

> But the love of Yahweh is from everlasting,
>   And to everlasting upon them that fear Him,
> And His righteousness unto children's children,
>   To them that remember His commandments to do
>   them."

(We may suspect that the " covenant-keepers " are a later gloss ; their introduction breaks into the regular metrical scheme of the Psalm.)

And so the whole feeling of the poet breaks out in the great demand for universal worship. Not only the speaker himself, but all other servants of Yahweh, human and superhuman, are called on to " bless " Yahweh. " Blessing " is not a mere synonym for " praise." It necessarily, to the Hebrew mind, involves the conveying to another person some spiritual power, vague and indefinable, perhaps, but none the less real. Words may make a difference, and more than once in the Old Testament we have illustrations of the desire survivors feel for some " blessing " from the dying, the release of a power which may be to their advantage. Implied in the demand that men and angels should " bless " Yahweh is the thought that even He can receive something of value from the little human soul, and the least that the inferior creature can do in recompense for all that he has received is to consecrate his own spiritual force, feeble though it may be, to the God who has given so much.

So, with sin forgiven and love assured, the worshipping soul can enter into the full joy of the presence of God. In fellowship with Him there are no fears, even when the traveller passes through the " valley of deepest gloom." Yahweh is a sun and a shield, in His presence there is fulness of joy, and at His right hand there are pleasures forevermore.

IX

PROVERBS

THERE seems to be in the human mind an ineradicable
instinct for what we call philosophy. Men have a
tendency to group events together and try to correlate
them with one another, seeing, as far as possible, a common principle at work in them. " Natural Science "
deals with the structure and behaviour of the physical
universe, and reduces the phenomena which it observes
to the smallest possible number of " natural laws "—
the phrase is popularly used, though the term " law " is
not strictly accurate. Chemical research first reduced
all forms of matter to " elements " and " atoms," the
atoms of different elements being different from one
another. It then went further and reduced the atoms to
their component parts, finding that the " electrons "
of one atom were identical with those of every other. It
thus gave a uniform explanation, in the last resort, for
the substance of which the universe is composed. Such
widely varying phenomena as the tides, the fall of a pin,
day and night, the seasons, are now explained by reference to a common and invariable principle called " the
law of gravitation."

The physical universe, however, does not exhaust the
range of experience. Emotion, thought, reason, and
other " spiritual " phenomena are not to be wholly
explained by reference to matter and its behaviour.
It is in metaphysical speculation that an attempt is made
to unify all experience, and to correlate both the material

and the non-material elements. In the last resort a
" monism " is the ultimate of all philosophical thinking.

But it necessarily begins in a very simple and humble
fashion. A small group of facts may be taken and covered
by a generalisation. Weather and climate, which are of
supreme importance to organised human life, have been
studied generation after generation, and men's experience
is apt to crystallize itself in such statements as that which
tells us that if the oak comes into leaf before the ash,
then the summer's rain will be but a splash, while if the
order is reversed, then the land will have a " soak."
Successive meteorological observations have led men to
say :

> " A rainbow at night
> Is the shepherd's delight ;
> A rainbow in the morning
> Is the shepherd's warning."

—a conclusion reached by experience long before
science was able to give a reason which linked the facts
with other observed phenomena. The same principle
was applied to other types of experience, and we have all
heard sayings like "A stitch in time save nine," a general
principle which we accept without necessarily endorsing
its mathematical accuracy. Such summaries of experience are usually couched in a form which makes them
easy to remember, and we often have to admit that they
appear to be based on an inadequate survey of the field.
We may even get " proverbs " which contradict each
other. Does absence make the heart grow fonder ?
Or is a person out of sight also out of mind ? People who
accept " proverbs " as expressions of ultimate truth may
take their choice. Or they may insist on modifying one
of the expressions and saying that absence makes a fond
heart fonder—an obvious accommodation to the other

" proverb " which goes far towards reducing the value of the first.

Such proverbs, then, may be described as the first tentative efforts of the human mind in the direction of a philosophy, and they are to be found almost everywhere. Regarded as the essence of human wisdom by generation after generation, they were quoted in market and field, in the city and in the open pasture. Learned men delighted in making collections of them, and it is interesting to note how often we find similar proverbs among peoples so far distant from one another as to preclude the idea of direct borrowing. That there was such borrowing from time to time is extremely probable—indeed, in some cases practically certain, but it is only when we get correspondence between fairly long groups of proverbs that we can adopt this theory.

Ancient Israel was no exception to the general rule. In reading the Old Testament we are met again and again by " proverbs," some of them apparently springing out of historical events, and others of a more general character. Sometimes more than one event is indicated as the origin of a proverb ; the saying " Is Saul also among the prophets? ", for example, is explained twice, once in I Sam. 10 : 12 and once in I Sam. 19 : 24. Collections were made, and, with other literature of a reflective or speculative type, were classed under the general head of " Wisdom "—the nearest term the ancient Hebrew had to " Philosophy." The proverb itself was a form of " mashal," a word whose exact significance is extremely elusive. To judge from comparative philology, its primary sense was that of " likeness " or " similarity," and the corresponding term is used in Arabic as a preposition meaning " like." But metaphor and simile are very far from exhausting the forms of expression to which the Hebrew word is applied. It is not used, for example, of Jotham's "parable" in Jud. 9 : 8-15. On the other hand it is employed to describe the great taunt-song over the fall of a tyrant, which we find in Is. 14 : 4 ff. In the Book of Job the speeches which begin with 27 : 1 and 29 : 1 are described by this word. So also Balaam's utterances in Nu. 23 and 24. In Ps. 44 : 14 and Job 17 : 6 it is rendered " byword," and the same sense may be read into the word " proverb " in such passages as Dt. 28 : 37, I Ki. 9 : 7, and Jer. 24 : 9. Any one who can give us an adequate explanation, and correlate all these different senses will have contributed in no small degree to our understanding of Hebrew psychology.

In the book which bears the name of " Proverbs," however, the type is, on the whole, fairly uniform. For the most part we have a collection—or rather several collections—of short, pithy, epigrammatic utterances, each of which aims at giving the results of experience in tabloid form. There are more extended sections which seem to be much nearer to the essay than to any other form of modern literature. One of these is an alphabetic poem in praise of the good woman, and offers an inter-esting picture of the social ideals of Israel. The actual form of the individual proverb is verse ; proverbs every-where tend to take this shape, since it is at once more im-pressive and easier to remember. The compilers made no effort, however, to produce actual poems, except in one or two instances where we seem to have something of the nature of a treatise. They were contented with gathering together a number of the sayings, sometimes arranging them in little groups dealing with the same subject, but taking little or no trouble to produce anything like a connected system of behaviour.

A superficial glance at the book shews that it was itself

a compilation of several collections, each with its own title. These are :

I. 1-9. Proverbs of Solomon.

II. 10 : 1-22 : 16. Proverbs of Solomon.

III. 22 : 17-24 : 22. Words of the Wise.

IV. 24 : 23-34. Additional words of the Wise.

V. 25-29. Proverbs of Solomon collected by the men of Hezekiah.

VI. 30. The words of Agur, son of Yakeh the Massaite.

VII. 31 : 1-9. The words of Lemuel, king of Massa, which his mother taught him.

VIII. 31 : 10-31. The virtuous woman. (This has no separate title, but its form and substance make it clear that it was originally an independent piece.)

It is clearly hopeless to try to date individual proverbs. Sayings handed from one to another may exist for centuries before they are written down or taken into a collection. Sometimes we may get hints from language or some other feature which may give us a clue to the general period at which a saying reached its present form, but such opportunities are rare in the greater part of the book as we now have it. The age in which a particular collection was made may be less baffling. We may, for example, accept the statement at the head of collection V, which tells us that the following proverbs were collected by the men of Hezekiah. Collection I, from its language and, still more from indications of an advancing metaphysical thought, may well be placed later than most of the book. The names of Lemuel and Agur seem to be purely artificial; no kingdom of " Massa " is known. It is worth noting that no collection is actually ascribed to Solomon, though the proverbs in the two largest sections are claimed as being his. He certainly had a reputation for epigrammatic speech, and may have been the first to formulate some of the sayings we now have before us. We have no more justification for believing that all " Solomonic proverbs " were uttered by David's successor than we have for supposing that all " ships of Tarshish " actually voyaged to the Atlantic coast of Spain. It is quite impossible to assign to him—or, indeed, to any other single author—a particular verse or group of verses in the book.

On internal grounds the first section, chs. 1–9, may be regarded as comparatively late. Unlike most of the book, it contains little that can be classed as typical " proverb " writing, and consists rather of a series of exhortations. The speaker is sometimes an aged sage who has learnt by experience and observation what is safe and profitable, and urges the young pupil to follow his advice. Sometimes the lessons are put into the mouth of Wisdom herself, who is personified in a fashion unique in the Old Testament. We are met with repeated exhortations to accept the teaching offered, e.g., in 1 : 2 ff, 2 : 1 ff, 3 : 1 ff, 4 : 1 ff, 20 ff, 5 : 1 ff, 6 : 20 ff, 9 : 10 ff. A cynical mind might suspect that in ancient times a teacher sometimes had difficulty in securing the attention and obedience of his pupils. The exhortations are reinforced by promises of all manner of benefits ; divine favour, honour among men, personal dignity, long life, quiet happiness, guidance and defence against temptation are among the benefits which will be assured to the wise youth. It is remarkable that great wealth is not stressed ; indeed it is hardly mentioned, and the learner is told that wisdom is a far more valuable possession than gold or precious stones (cf. 8 : 10 f). At the same time, warnings are given of the dangers into which a man may fall if he neglects the advice and instruction given to him. If he will not do as he is told, then disaster is certain, and he need expect no sympathy when it comes. Wisdom herself will mock at him and gloat over his calamities (1 : 26 ff).

So much space is given to these exhortations that we have in this section comparatively little direct advice. Piety, the right relation to God, is emphasised, the term used being "fear." This, of course, needs to be understood from the Hebrew point of view. It is seldom that words can be found in any two languages whose meaning exactly coincides, and emotions are often differently classified in the Hebrew and English minds. "Fear" is often far from being terror, or anything like it. It may be no more than anxiety or worry. The Hebrew says "fear not" when English would be content with "Do not worry about that." The feeling which seems to be common to all its uses is that of which men are conscious when they find themselves in the presence of something or of someone who is not wholly intelligible to them or is much greater than they. It is quite consistent with a happy confidence in the person who is "feared," though it demands that the inferior shall take into due consideration the personality and wishes of the superior. The "Fear of Yahweh," then, sums up in itself the attitude which the religious man will assume towards the object of his worship ; as has been well said, it is, perhaps, the nearest phrase in Hebrew to that which we call "religion." It may be as well to remember the insistence on this demand for a right attitude to God when we find ourselves dealing with other aspects of the teaching given in this book.

We have two or three instances of direct advice. Do

good to others when they are in need, and do it promptly
and cheerfully (3 : 27-28), do not injure him or quarrel
with him—if you can help it (3 : 29-30). Do not be
lazy (6 : 6 ff), but take the industrious ant as your model.
Be very careful to avoid backing somebody else's bills,
and if you do find that you have been trapped into doing
so, then spare no effort to get free (6 : 1 ff). In 6 : 16-19
we have a little collection of things that are offensive to
God. Such small catalogues are a favourite device with
the proverb-maker, and others occur in later collections.
The list given here is interesting. It includes pride,
falsehood, bloodshed, intrigue, malice in action, slander
and the stirring up of strife among brethren—an in-
structive commentary on the general state of social life
in ancient Israel.

One type of offence, however, is particularly condemned. That is the abuse of sex-relations. It is to
be noted that the main responsibility is laid upon the
woman. This may be due to a masculine prejudice
which was not uncommon in the ancient world, but it
may also suggest a state of society in which women
were so far secluded that seduction by a man was difficult
and almost impossible unless the woman herself had out-
raged the proprieties and taken the initiative. We
observe, too, that she is called the " strange " woman
(2 : 16), the word used meaning properly a foreigner. It
appears to be assumed that no true Israelite woman
would behave in this fashion. The subject is introduced
four or five times and as a rule only two or three verses
are given to it. The teacher is content to warn the
pupil that yielding to this temptation may give a
momentary pleasure, but can end only in destruction
and in death. But once we have a more extended
picture (7 : 5-23), not without a touch of a grim humour,

of the woman's methods in seduction. Again we get the feeling that she is necessarily the prime mover in the offence ; her male victim is " among the simple ones, . . . a young man void of understanding." In this case she is a married woman, who takes advantage of her husband's absence on a long journey to commit indiscriminate adultery. We can hardly avoid the impression that such conduct was far from being unknown in the writer's day, and formed one of the major social problems of his age.

The most striking and significant feature of this section, however, is the place given to Wisdom herself. She is personified as a teacher in several places, but her position is, in fact, much higher than this. She appears as a divine quality, and indeed, as something more than a quality. She is the actual agent of creation : " Yahweh by Wisdom hath founded the earth ; by Understanding hath He established the heavens " (3 : 19). That this is something more than pointing out the intelligence lying behind the universe is apparent from the more extended passage in 8 : 22 ff. Here Wisdom is a real person, " gotten " long before the creation of the world, when she stood " beside Him as a master-workman." Further, it is Wisdom who is in direct contact with humanity. The two great problems of religion are "How did God create the world ? " and " How does God come into contact with man ? " The answer given to both is " Through Wisdom," and the conception clearly approximates to that of a hypostasis. In other words it forms an early step towards a doctrine developed by Philo of Alexandria under the name " Logos," and fulfilled in the Christian acceptance of Jesus as the Eternal Son within the Godhead.

It is with the second section, much the longest in the

book, that we reach a typical collection of proverbs. It is difficult to see any kind of system or principle governing the arrangement of these sentences. For the most part each stands alone, and must be treated by and for itself. Not infrequently we find the same proverb more than once, a fact which suggests that we have here a compilation made from a number of smaller collections. On the other hand there are places in the later collections where a sentence is repeated within a few verses, and though this may be due to an error in copying, it is more likely that we should attribute it to the compiler himself. Thus we find exactly the same form in 14 : 12 and in 16 : 25, while more than once we have proverbs which are very similar, being identical in one part and differing only slightly in the other. Thus both 10 : 15 and 18 : 11 begin with the words " The rich man's wealth is his strong city," but in the one case the second half runs, " The destruction of the poor is their poverty," and in the the other, " And as an high wall in his own conceit." Examples of this kind of overlapping might be multiplied, and proverbial literature everywhere has examples of sayings in alternative forms.

It will often be felt that individual proverbs are based on an imperfect observation, or on an inadequate survey of the field with which they profess to deal. This is only natural and is partly due to the psychological effect which a proverb must produce if it is to be successful. It will fail to be impressive or to be remembered unless it has some direct appeal to mind or ear. Words are often chosen because they have a kind of assonance with one another. We may even find direct contradiction ; to take an example from a later section of this book we find in Prov. 26 : 4 an injunction not to answer a fool according to his folly, while the next verse gives exactly the opposite advice. Sound reasons are given in each case. But, taken as a whole, the maxims preserved in Proverbs do offer guidance to a reasonably satisfactory experience of life.

It is one thing to lay down rules for conduct, and quite another to give such reasons as will induce the hearer or reader to adopt them in practice. It is here that we feel the greatest weakness of the proverbs to lie. In the prophetic utterances we have the stern and uncompromising demand that men shall do the will of God. True, the inspired messengers seldom fail to warn us against the disasters which will follow inevitably on the disregard of moral principles. But that is not the chief motive in their minds. It is enough for them that God has laid down the law ; the duty of man is to obey it, whatever the consequences may be. In the Gospel we have the same ethical passion for righteousness, with an even clearer statement of the consequences, and here it is often pointed out that obedience to the will of God may entail suffering. The true disciple must carry a cross about with him ; he may well have to use it, and had better have it where it will be available at a moment's notice. The spirit of the Cross is not wholly absent from the Old Testament, and we may find examples of it in the matrimonial experience of Hosea, in the undeserved suffering of the perfect Servant, or in the fidelity of Job. But we miss this high note of sacrifice and surrender to principle when we read the Book of Proverbs. Goodness is commended less for its own sake than for the advantages which it brings in its train. The appeal is to a " cool self-love," not to an external object or ideal. " If you want to be happy, you had better be good " is the general principle which seems to underlie the great majority of the sayings. It is noticeable that many deal with matters of behaviour and manners rather than with high ethical truth. " The less said the better," " *Si tacuisses, philosophus mansisses*," " Even a fool when he holdeth his peace is accounted wise " (Prov. 17 : 28).—Very good advice but hardly inspiring to nobility of heart. Sometimes a deeper note is struck, and we come across utterances with the quality of " The heart knoweth its own bitterness ; and a stranger doth not intermeddle with its joy." (14 : 10).

This is not to say that religion is ignored. On the contrary a large number of the proverbs can come only from minds to which the reality and presence of God are primary facts of experience. Again and again the urgency of the right conduct is emphasised by the appeal to religion. The prudential motive is still present, as a rule, but there is at least the full acknowldgement of God as the supreme and righteous governor of human life. " The fear of Yahweh prolongeth days ; but the years of the wicked shall be shortened " (10 : 27), " The way of Yahweh is a strong hold to the upright ; but destruction shall be to the workers of iniquity " (10 : 29), " The fear of Yahweh is a fountain of life, to depart from the snares of death " (14 : 27), " Better is a little with the fear of Yahweh than great treasure and trouble therewith " (15 : 16), " The fear of Yahweh is the instruction of wisdom, and before honour is humility " (15 : 33), " The name of Yahweh is a strong tower ; the righteous runneth into it and is safe " (18 : 10)—these and many like them illustrate the doctrine that religion is profitable in this world. Sometimes we meet with a remark which shews a more complete insight into the real value of God's friendship, and occasionally we are reminded of a genuinely prophetic attitude. The futility of mere sacrifice, for example, finds expression in passages like

15 : 8—" The sacrifice of the wicked is an abomination unto Yahweh : but the prayer of the upright is his delight." Very similar is 21 : 27—" The sacrifice of the wicked is an abomination ; how much more when he bringeth it with a wicked mind," and in v. 3 of the same chapter we have a sentence which embodies one of the constant elements in prophetic teaching—" To do justice and judgement is more acceptable to Yahweh than sacrifice." Occasionally, however, we get the impression that some people value sacrifice as a means of getting a good meal, for it must be remembered that the ordinary sacrifice, as opposed to the burnt offering, gave only comparatively small portions of the victim to the altar and to the priests, while the bulk of the carcase was eaten by the worshipper. This is the explanation of expressions like that which meets us in 17 : 1 " Better is a dry morsel and quietness therewith, than a house full of sacrifices with strife." One of the attractions offered to the simple youth by the adulteress of ch. 7, comes under this head ; she tells her victim, " I have peace offerings with me ; this day have I payed my vows " (v. 14): in other words, she will give him a really good dinner.

In spite, however, of these occasional flights into higher strata, the general level of the religious impulse is that in which it pays to keep on the right side of God. One of the reasons is that it is impossible to escape from His all-seeing eye. " The eyes of Yahweh are in every place, keeping watch upon the evil and the good " (15 : 3). Indeed, the divine knowledge goes deeper than speech and action, the only criteria available to a man's fellows. " The fining pot is for silver, and the furnace for gold : but Yahweh trieth the hearts " (17 : 3), and we may go even further and say that God knows us far better than we know ourselves—" All the ways of a man are clean his own eyes, but Yahweh weigheth the spirits." (16 : 2). All this is perfectly true, and would be endorsed by every serious believer, whether he be one of the Biblical writers or no, but we miss the atmosphere of intimate friendship of which we are conscious, for example, in Ps. 139. Proverbs are essentially the wisdom of the ordinary man, not of the lofty or saintly mind.

Granted the limitations in spirit and outlook, we shall find in this book abundant evidence of sound common sense, and may get glimpses of the social life and standards of ancient Israel. The most conspicuous single figure is that of the fool, who disregards all maxims alike of religion, of ethics and of manners. There may be grades of folly, indicated by the use of different words, ranging from the simpleton who means no harm but is supremely gullible, to the deliberate and calculating villain, whose folly leads him to set himself in direct opposition to the will of God. In the last resort, all sin is folly, and in the more advanced grades the terms " fool " and "wicked" are practically synonymous. But we need not dwell on this type of person ; he will meet us on every page of this book.

The picture of family life drawn for us, albeit unintentionally, by the proverb-maker, is simple and charming. Great stress is laid on the relation between the parent and the child. The first proverb in this collection runs " A wise son maketh a glad father ; but a foolish son is the heaviness of his mother " (10 : 1). Closely allied is 15 : 20, " A wise son maketh a glad father ; but a foolish son despiseth his mother." Affection may be taken for granted, but more is required ; there must be respect and deference as well. Few if any blessings are more to be desired than a good family, and we feel that this is not merely due to the passion common to all orientals to have some one who will perpetuate their line and name after they are gone. " Children's children are the crown of old men ; and the glory of children are their fathers " (17 : 6). We hear more of the calamity due to a son's folly than we do of the delight given by a wise child. So " He that begetteth a fool doeth it to his sorrow : and the father of a fool hath no joy " (17 : 21). " A foolish son is a grief to his father, and bitterness to her that bare him " (17 : 25). There may even be cases in which the child betrays violent animosity, and this is one of the deadliest sins : " Whoso curseth his father or his mother, his lamp shall be put out in blackest darkness " (20 : 20). At times we are reminded that we are in the midst of a society in which slavery was normal, though on a comparatively mild basis ; the slave has to be regarded as a member of the household, and may even rise to sonship : " A wise slave shall have rule over a son that causeth shame, and shall have part of the inheritance among the brethren " (17 : 2). One of the regular parental duties is education in the widest sense, and Israel shared with the rest of the ancient world the view that the process of learning was always painful. It becomes the child to accept with submission the correction and instruction of his father : " A wise son heareth his father's instruction ; but a scorner heareth not rebuke " (13 : 1). " Chasten thy son for there is hope," i.e., if he be duly punished (19 : 18). Best known of all such sayings is that of 13 : 24 : " He that spareth his rod hateth his son : but he that loveth him chasteneth him betimes." It is, after all, in early youth that a character is really formed : " Train up a child in the way he should go : and when he is old he will not depart from it " (22 : 6).

For the most part, little is said in this section of Proverbs about women, but we get the impression that, though they played little part in public life, they occupied a position of authority in the home. Apart from a man's own character and actions, no influence had so great a bearing on his happiness or misery as did his wife. The key, perhaps, is struck by 18 : 22—" Whoso hath found a wife hath found good, and hath obtained favour of Yahweh." Again, "A gracious woman retaineth honour" (11 : 16). It is recognized that a good wife is a divine gift : "House and riches are the inheritance of fathers : but a prudent wife is from Yahweh (19 : 14). At the same time, it is realized that marriage is a lottery, and that a woman in the house is not necessarily a blessing. It is her tongue in particular that distresses her men folk, though there may be something deeper ; the fools are not all males. "A virtuous woman is a crown to her husband, but she that maketh ashamed is as rottenness in his bones " (12 : 4), " As a jewel of gold in a swine's snout, so is a fair woman which is without discretion " (11 : 22), " The contentions of a wife are a continual dropping " (19 : 13), " It is better to dwell in a corner of the housetop, than with a brawling woman in a wide house " (21 : 9), " It is better to dwell in the wilderness, than with a contentious and fretful woman " (21 : 19).

A good deal is said about the relations of men with one another outside the family. Kings appear from time to time, but they are rather remote from ordinary life, and have special duties and characteristics. We may fairly assume that what is said of them is valid for all rulers, whether they bore the royal title or not. A king's position is dependent on the size of the population over which he rules : " In the multitude of people is the king's splendour ; but in the want of people is the destruction of the prince (14 : 28). His authority is regarded as practically absolute, and it is exceedingly dangerous to offend him, while great advantage may accrue from his favour. " The king's favour is towards a wise servant : but his wrath is against him that causeth shame " (14 : 35), " The wrath of a king is as messengers of death : but a wise man will pacify it " (16 : 14). At the same time, even the king is subordinate to God : " The king's heart is in the hand of Yahweh, as the rivers of water : he turneth it whithersoever he will " (21 : 1). He has special abilities if he is a real king, the most important being that which can discern truth beneath the mass of falsehood which will normally be presented to him. This looks almost magical, " In the lips of the king is divination : his mouth transgresseth not in judgement " (16 : 10). The moral law is, if possible, more firmly binding on him than on any other, for it is his duty not only to keep it but to enforce it on others. " The abomination of kings " (i.e., that which is abominable in a king) " is to commit wickedness : for the throne is established in righteousness " (16 : 12), " A king that sitteth on the throne of judgement scattereth away all evil with his eyes " (20 : 8), " Righteous lips are the delight of kings ; and they love him that speaketh right" (16 : 13).

In his dealings with his fellows, a man is exhorted to maintain his self-control. " He that is slow to anger is better than the mighty ; and he that ruleth his spirit than he that taketh a city " (16 : 32), " The discretion of a man maketh him slow to anger ; and it is his glory to pass over a transgression " (19 : 11), " Whoso keepeth his mouth and his tongue keepeth his soul from troubles " (21 : 23). It will be noticed that prominence is given here to control over language, and more proverbs are devoted to foolish and dangerous speech than to any other specific type of action. At the same time, there are in it great possibilities for good. "The mouth of the righteous is a well of life : but violence covereth the mouth of the wicked" (10 : 11), "The tongue of the righteous is as choice silver : the heart of the wicked is little worth" (10 : 20), "The words of the wicked are an ambush for blood : but the mouth of the upright shall deliver them" (12 : 6), "The tongue of the wise useth knowledge aright : but the mouth of fools poureth out foolishness" (15 : 2), "The heart of him that hath understanding seeketh knowledge : but the mouth of fools feedeth on folly" (15 : 14), "A fool's lips enter into contention, and his mouth calleth for strokes. A fool's mouth is his destruction, and his lips are the snare of his soul" (18 : 6 f.). It must not be forgotten, however, that there may be more below the surface than appears on first hearing an utterance, for "the words of a man's mouth are as deep waters" (18 : 4).

In accordance with this view of human speech, we find that truthfulness takes a high place among the virtues. "Lying lips are an abomination to Yahweh : but they that deal truly are his delight" (12 : 22), "The desire of a man is his kindness : and a poor man is better than a liar" (19 : 22). This is most important in legal procedure, and the value of a reliable witness is, as everywhere in the east, very great, while perjury is so often denounced as to make us feel that it was far from uncommon. "A true witness delivereth souls, but a deceitful witness speaketh lies" (14 : 25), "A worthless witness maketh judgement a mockery : and the mouth of the wicked swalloweth iniquity" (19 : 28)—these are typical statements.

Closely allied is the common honesty of the market and the shop, which is mentioned more than once.

So in 11 : 1 we hear that " A false balance is an abomination unto Yahweh : but a just weight is his delight," while the offence of having " divers weights " is condemned in 20 : 10—" Divers weights and divers measures, both of them are alike abomination unto Yahweh," and the honest tradesman is commended in 16 : 11, " A just balance and scales are Yahweh's : all the weights of the bag are his work."

More proverbs are concerned with industry and laziness than with any other virtue and its corresponding vice. Particular stress is laid on the troubles which will inevitably meet the sluggard. If he will not take the trouble to till or reap his fields, he will be in danger of starvation, besides bringing disgrace on his family, for " The sluggard will not plough by reason of the cold ; therefore shall he beg in harvest and have nothing " (20 : 4), while, on the contrary, the industrious man will have his needs fully satisfied—" Love not sleep, lest thou come to poverty ; open thine eyes and thou shalt be satisfied with bread " (20 : 13). The effect on his parents is described in 10 : 5—" He that gathereth in summer is a wise son : but he that sleepeth in harvest is a son that causeth shame," He is useless to any employer : " As vinegar to the teeth, and as smoke to the eyes, so is the sluggard to them that send him " (10 : 26). There is a certain humour in some of these pictures, that, for instance, of the man who has energy enough to put his hand into the dish, but is too lazy to carry the food to his mouth (19 : 24), or of the man so hard put to it for an excuse for lying in bed instead of going to work that he makes the absurd remark, " There is a lion without, I shall be slain in the streets " (22 : 13).

Humility is another virtue strongly recommended. Pride is dangerous ; we may have here something of that feeling which lay behind the Greek theory of "hubris"—that arrogance which is produced by success, and will certainly lead to disaster. So "When pride cometh, then cometh shame : but with the lowly is wisdom" (11 : 2), and one of the most familiar of the proverbs is 16 : 18, "Pride goeth before destruction, and an haughty spirit before a fall." The reason for this is to be found in the fact that God will not tolerate any self-exaltation on man's part : "An high look, and a proud heart, and the lamp of the wicked is sin" (21 : 4), or, more explicitly, "Every one that is of a proud heart is an abomination to Yahweh : though hand join in hand he shall not be unpunished" (16 : 5).

Pride and arrogance may be expected more particularly in the attitude taken by the rich towards the poor, and a good deal is said on this aspect of social life . Attempts are made to decry the value of wealth ; it is of no real use to man, and there are many things which are more desirable. So in 11 : 28 we read : "He that trusteth in his riches shall fall : but the righteous shall flourish as a branch," and a similar idea underlies 13 : 7 —" There is that maketh himself rich, yet hath nothing : there is that maketh himself poor, yet hath great wealth." Far superior is religion : "Better is a little with the fear of Yahweh than great treasure and trouble therewith" (15 : 16), or morality : "Better is a little with righteousness than great revenues with injustice" (16 : 8), or wisdom : "How much better is it to get wisdom than gold ! Yes, to get understanding is rather to be chosen than silver" (16 : 16), or quiet contentment : "Better is a dry morsel, and quietness therewith, than an house full of sacrifices with strife" (17 : 1).

Logically, such an attitude to wealth should mean that there is no reason why the poor should not be as much honoured as the rich, and as well treated. It goes without saying that generosity is greatly to be desired, for, however much the poor are to be respected, they are still in need. Poverty has serious disadvantages. It is difficult for the pauper to keep his friends in a world where the decisive social factor is money : " Wealth maketh many friends ; but the poor is separated from his friend " (19 : 4). The man with no property is exposed to the domination and even the oppression of his wealthier fellows : " The rich ruleth over the poor, and the borrower is servant to the lender " (22 : 7), " The poor useth entreaties ; but the rich answereth roughly " (18 : 23). Such conduct, of course, is a direct violation of all true religious principle, for " The rich and the poor meet together : Yahweh is the maker of them all " (22 : 2). On the other hand, humane treatment of the poor is a definitely religious act, though it has not yet risen to that unique place which almsgiving occupied in Pharisaic theology. Still : " He that oppresseth the poor insulteth his Maker, but he that hath mercy on the needy honoureth him " (14 : 31). Generosity to the destitute will earn a reward from Yahweh : " He that hath pity on the poor lendeth to Yahweh, and for his deed he will pay him in full " (19 : 17). The payment will be a fitting one, for " there is that scattereth and yet increaseth ; and there is that withholdeth more than is meet, but it tendeth to poverty " (11 : 24). It is dangerous not to relieve distress : " Whoso stoppeth his ears at the cry of the poor, he also shall cry himself, but shall not be heard " (21 : 13).

We have thus comparatively little said about some of the commoner vices. There is practically no mention of sexual offences, such as occupy so large a space in the first section of the book, and drunkenness is condemned only once (20 : 1). What does interest the sages whose words are here collected is the relation between man and God, including the attitude and behaviour of man to his neighbours. The two are not sharply distinguished in the minds of the speakers. It has been well said that the whole outlook of Proverbs is essentially religious and the thought of God is always present, even in sayings that appear to us to be purely secular. There is no escape from the fact that God is concerned with every aspect of human life, and will reward or punish as man's action may deserve. At the same time, it has to be admitted that we have a lower religious level than those of the prophet and mystic. The importance of piety and upright conduct lies in the fact that they are profitable ; God will see that they are rewarded. Violation of divine law, on the other hand, will lead inevitably to punishment. The whole drama must be played out on the stage of this life, and we have little reference even to She'ol. That means that every one can see for himself the working of Yahweh's law of retribution, and should take warning from it. These warnings have been gathered together, culled from long and varied human experience, and they have been set before us in this fashion. By following the lines laid down, any man may reasonably expect to live a quiet and inoffensive life, achieving a certain measure of worldly success, and that was an ideal not to be despised in an age when personal security was far less easily attainable than it is in the more highly organised society of our own day.

The next collection has no title in our present text, but there is a strong feeling that the phrase " Words of the wise " originally stood at the head of v. 17, and has been transferred to its present position by a copyist's error. The extent of the collection is not certain. The normal view is that it contains 22 : 17-24 : 22, but it has been suggested that a division should be made between 23 : 14 and 15. There is a fresh exhortation to obedience in 23 : 15, and the first part has one striking peculiarity to which allusion must be made later. The general character of the whole, however, is uniform, and for practical study of the book itself the two parts may be treated as a single whole.

What has been said about the subject matter of division II will apply equally well to section III. The same themes are treated, and there is no conspicuous variation in tone, outlook, or doctrine. The general social and religious background, too, shews no remarkable variation ; the sayings here come from the same order of society and from the same religious community as those at which we have already glanced. There is, however, one important difference in form. In nearly every case the proverbs contained in section II occupied only a single line each, and there was, as far as we can gather, little attempt at an organized arrangement. In section III, on the other hand, the proverbs are longer, containing two or three lines, in which the sense often runs on continuously. The same subject rarely appears more than once ; drunkenness, it is true, is condemned in 23 : 19-21 and in 23 : 29-31, and warnings against oppressing the poor occur in 22 : 22-23 and 23 : 10-11, but these are the only outstanding cases. At the same time, it is not easy to trace a formal and systematic arrangement, except that we may note the way in which the collector begins with an exhortation whose purpose is essentially religious. He puts God first, and his claim to a hearing is that his in-struction will lead men to trust in Yahweh.

There is one feature of this collection, however, which has attracted a great deal of attention. We have already observed that similar proverbs are likely to be found among peoples widely separated in space and time. There are many parallels to the sayings of the Jewish sages in the literature of Babylonia, Greece, and other peoples, some of the most obvious being found in the sayings of Ahikar, best known to us through an Aramaic papyrus of the fifth century B.C. But the closest parallels are to be found in Egyptian writings, which range from the third millennium B.C. to a comparatively late period. One of these, whose composition is commonly dated about 800 B.C. is known as " The Teaching of Amen em-ope." With the exception of 22 : 23, 26, 27, every verse in Proverbs 22 : 17—23 : 12 has a parallel in this Egyptian collection. Sometimes the sentences are extremely close ; the following may be noted in particular :

PROVERBS	AMEN-EM-OPE
22 : 17 Incline thine ear and hear my words, And apply thine heart to apprehend.	Give thine ear and hear what I say, And apply thine heart to apprehend.
22 : 20. Have I not written for thee thirty sayings Of counsels and knowledge ?	Consider these thirty chapters ; They delight, they instruct.
22 : 22. Rob not the poor because he is poor, Neither oppress the lowly in the gate.	Beware of robbing the poor And of oppressing the afflicted.
22 : 29. A man who is skilful in his business Shall stand before kings.	A scribe who is skilful in his business Findeth himself worthy to be a courtier.
23 : 4. Toil not to become rich.	Toil not after riches.
23 : 10. Remove not the widow's landmark, And enter not into the fields of the fatherless.	Remove not the landmark from the bounds of the field, Nor shift the position of the measuring-cord.

(Taken from Oesterley, Commentary on Proverbs, pp. xlvi. f. The text has been amended in places, and is almost certainly correct.)

The similarities are much too close to be accidental, though there are one or two points to be noted. The passages from Amen-em-ope are not taken from the same or consecutive sections, and, indeed, are sometimes widely separated. The Egyptian form is usually longer than the Hebrew, and sometimes several lines in the former correspond to a single one in the latter. In the third place, the sayings in Proverbs are adapted to a people who worshipped Yahweh, though without any belief in a valid life after death. It may, however, be doubted whether these divergences are sufficient to dispel the very strong impression that there has been direct borrowing on the one side or the other. It is not impossible that the debt is on the part of the Egyptian sage, who must, then, have known this collection much as it now stands. Here we have the evidence which has led to the impression that 22 : 17—23 : 14 once formed an independent booklet. Parallels with Amen-em-ope are to be found in many other places in Proverbs, but nowhere else are they so abundant ; indeed, taking the book as a whole, it has closer affinities with Ahikar than with any other known collection of wise sayings. While, then, the evidence is not absolutely conclusive, it is strong enough to make the theory of borrowing highly probable.

The fourth section is admittedly an appendix to the third, adding two or three subjects—justice, laziness and slander, which are not mentioned in the main body of the collection. It shares in all the characteristics of the preceding chapters, except the close parallels with Amen-em-ope ; the description of the sluggard and of his garden is one of the longest " proverbs " in the book.

Section V is dated in the reign of Hezekiah, i.e. towards the end of the eighth century B.C. There is no reason to question the accuracy of the title, except that it is hardly likely that Solomon was the author of all the proverbs contained in these chapters, though some of them may have been much older than the date of compilation. In general character it closely resembles section II, and from time to time we come across exact reproductions of sayings found in the former collection. Thus 25 : 24 is verbally identical with 21 : 9, and probably 27 : 13 with 20 : 16. The resemblance between 28 : 6 and 19 : 1 is so close—one speaks of a rich man and the other of fool—as to make original identity plausible. Similarities are to be found in many other places, e.g., in 27 :21 and 17 : 3, in 26 : 13 and 22 : 13, or in 26 : 15 and 19 : 24. There are occasional signs of some attempt to arrangement ; in 26 : 23-26, for example, we have a series of utterances dealing with hypocrites, and the two verses following speak of the proper retribution which falls on the evildoer. But, in general, all that has been said about section II will apply equally well to section V.

Ch. 30 gives us a new name, otherwise unknown. It is that of a certain Agur, who is, probably, indicated as a Massaite. Massa was the name of an Arab tribe. He opens in a fashion which has aroused some difference of opinion. His language is that of extreme humility, but some readers feel that he is being ironical, and that he really would claim to be wiser than all his fellows. On the whole the obvious meaning seems the more likely. The subjects with which he deals are already familiar, but he has one peculiarity. Nearly all his sayings are grouped in little sections, each of which is devoted to different things which illustrate a common principle. " There are two . . . three . . . four things which . . ." Thus in vv. 7-9 he asks for two things, truthfulness and a moderate share of this world's goods. One group seems to have lost its heading. It is that of vv.

11-14, which describes four types of wicked people. Apart from this feature, there is little to add to what has already been said about other collections.

Nine verses are devoted to Lemuel, called a king, who, again, is known only from this passage. He, too, is assigned to the tribe of Massa. It is possible that the compilers of the book were deliberately indicating the employment of some Arabian collection of proverbs, though it is a little strange that they should acknowledge their indebtedness only here. Lemuel has only two things to say, and both have been said before in this book. One is a warning against sexual offences and the other a vigorous condemnation of drunkenness. They are addressed expressly to kings, and the speaker is the mother of Lemuel.

The last section in the book is an acrostic poem on the virtuous woman. It is extremely interesting for the light it throws on the position of woman in the ancient Israelite community. She is able to take a considerable share in the business life of her time, though it is not clear what part she plays, except that she is in the habit of selling the products of her loom. While she does not seem to be secluded in the way respectable women are in so many parts of the east to-day, her main concern is within her house. Here she is the absolute mistress, and even her husband is mentioned only as praising her for her virtues, and for the position he takes among his fellows—apparently due to the excellence of his wife. She it is who is responsible for giving food and clothing to all the members of her household, including the slaves as well as the family droper. She belongs to a fairly well-to-do class, as is shewn by the people she employs, and the suggestion is that it is she who has succeeded in making this possible. What strikes us most in reading the poem is the woman's immense industry. She is at work by day and by night. She rises before dawn and prepares the first meal for the whole household, and far into the night she is at work with spindle and loom. It would seem that wool was bought direct from the growers, and that the whole process of manufacturing it was carried on in the home. At the same time she does not neglect her social duties, the first of which is caring for the poor about her. We have here a picture of energetic benevolence which offers us the ideal for the age from which it comes. Amos and Isaiah had fully recognized the fact that in the last resort it is the women who set the social and moral standards of the community, and their denunciations of what they saw form a strong contrast to this attractive picture. We cannot sum our impressions up better than in Oesterley's words : " The traditional beauty of Jewish home-life is both explained and illustrated by a passage like this, for we may well believe that the picture presented reflects what was a reality in many a Jewish home."

One question still remains before we leave the subject of Proverbs. What is their date ? As we have seen, it is quite hopeless even to attempt an answer in so far as the individual sayings are concerned, but it may be possible to get some idea of the approximate period at which the collections were made. The first section is almost certainly late. It has the character of a single piece of composition, and the thought, culminating in an advanced metaphysical conception of Wisdom, cannot be early. The two larger collections, on the other hand, may well have been made in the main before the exile, though we must allow for the possibility of modification in later times. The references to kings are not necessarily to Jewish kings, but it is more natural to interpret them in this way. The inscription at the head of ch. 25, according to which the collection was made in the eighth century, may well preserve a tradition which is substantially correct. In that case we may fairly assume that the other Solomonic collection is also pre-exilic. The " words of the wise," as we have seen, shew a close connection with Egyptian literature, and there is at least the possibility that Amen-em-ope knew of its existence. That would throw this collection also back well into the monarchical age. If, on the other hand, the Egyptian document is the original, then the earliest date for the Hebrew collection would be the time immediately preceding the exile, and it would probably have to be placed after the return. The theological position is interesting ; while there is no explicit doctrine of monotheism, it is clear that no other deity than Yahweh is considered—a phenomenon which might be due to post-exilic redaction. There is no doctrine of a valid life after death (a striking contrast to the Egyptian proverbial literature), and it is worth observing that we find nowhere a suggestion that such a theory had ever been propounded in Israel. Here we have another indication of a date which must not be carried down too far. But in the case of Proverbs, as in the Psalms, the actual date is quite unimportant, for their subject and their teaching are such as will appeal to human nature in every age.

X

THE SONG OF SONGS

In I Kings 4 : 32 it is said of Solomon " And he spake three thousand proverbs, and his songs were a thousand and five." Like his father, then, Solomon won from his contemporaries a great reputation as a poet, and it is not surprising that later generations were inclined to attribute to him, not only the proverbial sayings of the whole nation, but also a certain amount of its poetry. True, only one Psalm was ascribed to him (Ps. 72), and it is clear that men never thought of him as they did of David, but it was easy to regard him as one of the great figures in the story of Israel's secular poetry. Little enough of that poetry has survived ; we have an occasional snatch here and there, but the men to whom we owe the preservation of that fraction of Hebrew litera- ture which has come down to us were interested in religion first, last, and all the time. A piece of prose or verse had to prove its title to be called religious to justify its inclusion in the enduring corpus of ancient Israelite writings.

The matter was simpler in the case of the " Song of Songs," because the name Solomon occurs in the book some half dozen times. There was nothing strange to the ancient mind in a man's writing in the third person about himself, and who should be able to write better about the king than Solomon himself ? But a close study makes it practically impossible for us to accept this tradition, for reasons into which we may enter later.

We shall do well first of all to see what the book actually contains, and then we shall be in a better position to discuss matters of authorship and interpretation.

On the surface the book is composed of a number of short poems, some of them clearly mutilated, and others showing serious corruptions of text. They are all love poems, of that there can be no doubt, and in differentiating them we are guided by an important grammatical factor. Hebrew, like all Semitic languages, distinguished between the masculine and the feminine of the second person in its pronouns and verbs. It is thus in a large number of cases, possible for us to see whether a poem, or even a sentence, is addressed to a man or a woman. The sex of the speaker is often easily determined, and from time to time we have language put into the mouth of a group of people, though it is not necessarily clear whether they are male or female. We may analyse the book as follows :

1.	1 : 2-4.	A woman speaks to a man.
2.	1 : 5-6.	A woman speaks to a company, probably of women.
3.	1 : 7-8.	A woman speaks to a man, and is answered by him.
4.	1 : 9-11.	A man speaks to a woman.
5.	1 : 12-14.	A woman speaks to a man.
6.	1 : 15-17.	A man speaks to a woman, and is answered by her.
7.	2 : 1-7.	A woman speaks to a company of women.
8.	2 : 8-14.	A woman speaks.
9.	2 : 15.	A man speaks (?) (apparently a fragment only).
10.	2 : 16-17.	A woman speaks to a man.
11.	3 : 1-5.	A woman speaks to a company of women.
12.	3 : 6-8.	A short piece describing a woman coming in state from the wilderness.
13.	3 : 9-11.	A company of women is summoned to look at Solomon, coming in procession.

14. 4 : 1-7.   A man speaks to a woman (probably there are two pieces here).

15. 4 : 8-11.   A man speaks to a woman.

16. 4 : 12-5 : 1. A man speaks to a woman, who replies in the latter part of 4 : 16.

17. 5 : 2-6 : 3. Dialogue between a woman and a company of women.

18. 6 : 4-9.   A man speaks to a woman.

19. 6 : 10.   A company speak (?) (apparently a fragment).

20. 6 : 11-12.   A woman speaks.

21. 6 : 13-7 : 5. A company (of women ?) speak to a woman.

22. 7 : 6-9.   A man speaks to a woman.

23. 7 : 10.   A woman speaks (a fragment ?).

24. 7 : 11-13.   A woman speaks to a man.

25. 8 : 1-3.   A woman speaks to a man. (8 : 4 probably introduced by accident.)

26. 8 : 5-7.   A woman speaks to a man, following on an enquiry by others.

27. 8 : 8-10.   Brothers speak of their sister, who takes up their last remarks.

28. 8 : 11-12.   Solomon's vineyard.

29. 8 : 13-14.   A man speaks and is answered by a woman.

On the surface, then, the book consists of a number of love poems, or parts of love poems. Two questions naturally arise. One is as to whether it is to be regarded as a single whole, into which all the parts fit, or whether it is only an anthology. The other is as to the interpretation to be placed on the whole. In part the two questions may overlap ; if it be a consistent unity, then the interpretation will necessarily be affected.

As we read this book, we feel that we fully understand the difficulty the Jewish Rabbis are said to have met when they sought to give it a place in Scripture. Tradition says that it, together with Ecclesiastes, was admitted only after the fall of Jerusalem in A.D. 70. The name of Solomon gave it a certain title, but the saints and sages of Judaism could hardly include in their sacred literature a work which dealt wholly with secular love.   The problem was solved by the theory that it was an allegory from start to finish, and that it really gave a picture of the love existing between Yahweh and the ideal Israel.   The same problem faced the Christian Church, and it was not alleviated by the tendency to monasticism, which placed love between man and woman on a comparatively low level, and regarded marriage as an inferior state to celibacy.   The example of Jewish scholars, however, afforded a precedent, and for centuries the book was held to be a parable of the mutual love between Christ and His Church—a view which is still represented in the chapter headings of many modern Bibles.

The general outlook of modern scholarship, going back to the earlier part of the nineteenth century, was unable to accept an allegorical explanation of the book, and tried to explain it as a purely secular poem.   It was still held to be a unity, due to a single author, and the favourite method of treatment was to describe it as a drama. Solomon, the great lover, was on royal progress through northern Israel, and, passing through the village of Shunem, observed a maiden of extraordinary beauty. He wooed her in the guise of a shepherd and had her brought to his harem, eventually winning her love. This scheme left certain points unexplained, and seemed in some ways to be forced until it was modified by the introduction of a third character.   The new view followed the old up to the point at which the maiden was taken to Jerusalem, but it gave her a rustic lover in her old home to whom she had been betrothed.   The king used all his arts, but in vain ; the girl remained true to her old love, and in the end Solomon yielded, and generously sent her back to her home, where the faithful couple were reunited.

It would be going too far to say that a romantic story of this kind would have been quite impossible in ancient Israel. We have too small a fragment of Israelite literature in our hands to make so dogmatic a statement. But we can say that, apart from this book, there is not the slightest evidence for its existence. There are plenty of instances of deep affection and even of passionate love between men and women—who can forget the story of Hosea? But we have nowhere else any suggestion of a literature surrounding this aspect of human relations. Matrimony is usually much more a *mariage de convenance*, and where it is described it is cited because of its influence on family or national fortunes. It may, however, be fairly answered that such a literature, if it existed, would hardly have been likely to survive.

The case against the dramatic form is more serious. We have good reason to believe that drama did exist in ancient Israel, as among the surrounding peoples. We have abundant evidence for it both from Babylonia and from northern Syria, and from time to time we meet with passages in the Old Testament which suggest very strongly that similar drama was to be found in Israel also. But this drama was always essentially religious, and was, indeed, intimately bound up with the cultus. The New Year festival, for example, in Mesopotamia involved a mimic representation of the great war among the gods which preceded the foundation of the earth as we know it. Its leading characters were Tiamat and Marduk, and the so-called Creation epic formed a part of it. So in northern Syria we have the annual representation of the death, rebirth and marriage of the fertility-god, forming a ritual whose magical effect is to secure prosperity for the coming year. But nowhere have we any evidence of a drama outside the cultic system.

It is true that our Israelite literature is very scanty, but that of Mesopotamia is abundant, and we should almost certainly have found some reference to secular drama if it had existed in Babylonia or within the knowledge of the Babylonians. Drama developed in Greece from a rude form of cultus, but we can trace the process, and we have no right to assume that a parallel course was followed in the Semitic world. Compared with this objection the entire absence of anything approaching stage directions is a minor difficulty, though it leaves room for a high degree of imagination and, possibly, of ingenuity.

The theory of a secular drama, then, has been largely abandoned. But an interpretation has been offered which brings the Song of Songs into close connection with the religious drama of the ancient world. It has been noted that many of the phrases used and of the ideas involved are characteristic of the fertility cult common to practically all western Asia in ancient times. In particular the worship of Ishtar is cited for parallels—the dove, for example, is the bird sacred to this goddess. She was known in many parts under different names— Ishtar, Astarte, Ashtoreth are all forms of the same word. She is also the Aphrodite of Cyprus and the Levant generally, and the Artemis of Ephesus. No cult was more widely spread in the ancient world than hers, especially after her identification with the Egyptian Isis. Normally her worship involved the sacred marriage to which reference has already been made, and room was often left for gross and licentious rites. It has been suggested that we have in the Song of Songs a Hebrew version of the libretto for a ritual performed in honour of Ishtar. Naturally it could not have been accepted as such by correct post-exilic Judaism, but it might have survived in northern Israel, and copies of the text might have found their way to the south long after the original meaning and purpose had been forgotten.

A hypothesis of this kind is as difficult to refute as it is to demonstrate. The list of words known to be common to the Ishtar cult and to the Song of Songs is impressive, though most of them may quite well have been used in other connections. All we can say for certain is that if this view be correct, the origin of the book must have been long forgotten before it could even have been considered in the orthodox Judaism of the post-exilic age.

One other line of interpretation deserves mention. It is held in some quarters that the marriage customs of modern Syria (which may go back to very ancient times) afford a clue to the nature and purpose of the book. The festal season lasts for a week, and during that time the bride and bridegroom are hailed and treated as king and queen. Their throne is the threshing-sledge, a heavy structure of wooden boards forming a small platform, studded with nails and stones on its under side. Its normal use is to be dragged by oxen over the corn on the threshing floor. It was certainly one of the implements in common use from the earliest times, and we hear of it in II Sam. 24 : 22, Is. 28 : 27, 41 : 15, Am. 1 : 3. A seat is placed on it for the wedding ceremony, and the young couple are drawn in state wherever they have to go. The ritual is sometimes elaborate, and includes various interludes such as a sword dance, in which the bride protects herself against her lover by whirling a sword before her. She may sometimes cut him severely with it, though as a rule she is not too severe in her defence. It is at least possible that similar procedure was current in ancient Palestine, though direct evidence is lacking. But practically every piece contained in the Song of Songs can be fitted into the scheme. At the same time, such attempts as have been made to reconstruct the ritual from the Song have to place the various portions in a different order from that in which the book itself presents them.

The plain fact is that any attempt to find a consistent thread running through the book, with whatever interpretation we may seek to place on it, must depend to a large extent on imaginative conjecture. All we can say for certain is that we have a collection of erotic lyrics, most of them short and some mutilated—in a few instances we seem to have only a single line. The same phrase or sentence may occur more than once ;

> " I adjure you,
>   Ye daughters of Jerusalem,
>   By the roes and by the hinds of the field,
>   That ye stir not up, nor awaken
>   Love till it please."

This is in 2 : 7 and 3 : 5, and, with slight variation, in 8 : 4, though it is hardly in place in this last context. The last verse of the book runs :

> " Flee, my beloved,
>   And be like a roe,
>   Or a young hart
>   On the mountains of spices."

Here we have a verse which is almost identical with 2 : 17; the differences may easily be explained by textual corruption. These and similar facts suggest the same kind of structure which we find so often in the prophetic books, a collection of independent short pieces, sometimes put together almost haphazard, though there are instances where the compiler's motive may be guessed. Thus the picture of the woman coming attended by a stout company of swordsmen (3 : 6-8) is immediately followed by a description of " Solomon's " gorgeous travelling litter. The two pieces 6 : 13-7 : 5 and 7 : 6-9 both speak of a woman's beauty, though the speakers are not the same.

The pieces are of varied character. Some are descriptions of the physical beauty of the beloved, man or woman. In 4 : 1-7, for example, and in 7 : 6-9 the suitor gives pictures of the woman he loves, while in 6 : 13–7 : 5 we have a more intimate account of her charms. Here the girl has been asked to reveal herself to a company of people, almost certainly other women, and they find no fault or blemish of any kind in her. If the marriage theory be correct, this may indicate one feature of the proceedings ; such inspection of a bride by older women has parallels elsewhere, though we should have to go far before finding anything exactly similar. In 5 : 10-16 the position is reversed, and the woman gives a description of her lover, in answer to a request by a company of women. This piece forms a part of a longer poem, and it is possible that originally those already mentioned may have been extracted from more extensive narratives. In a few cases we have little idylls. In 1 : 7-8, for instance, the fair shepherdess—or rather goatherd—seeks to enjoy her swain's company during the noonday rest. But she wishes to avoid the possibility of being insulted by his ruder fellows, and he gives her directions as to how he may be found. Twice we have stories of nocturnal adventures, which may be regarded rather as dreams than as records of actual events. The two are in some ways similar, though they end very differently. In the one case (3 : 1-5) the girl rises to seek her lover, asks the city watchmen if they have seen him, and soon afterwards finds him and brings him to her mother's home. In the other (5 : 2-8)—which is more obviously a dream—he himself comes to the house and asks her to come out with him. After a protest against being taken out she consents, but when she leaves the house the man is gone. Again we have the watchmen, but this time they maltreat her, and she appeals to a company of women for help in finding him. The form of the poem suggests that she may have been telling them her dream, for it is somewhat strange to meet a company of women in the streets of an eastern city by night. They ask her to describe him and she gives the account which we have already mentioned. Then they ask what are his habits, that they may know where to look for him, and are told that he feeds his flock among the "lilies," a word which probably indicates the scarlet anemone so common in Palestine.

Many of the pieces are concerned with the delight the lovers have in one another's society. Particularly noticeable is their pleasure in being together in the outdoor world. The songs carry us into the springtime of the year, into lovely mountain scenery, and into gardens beautiful with flowers and fragrant with spices. The background is that of a people whose work lies primarily with flocks of goats and sheep, and we have only occasional references to agriculture proper. We miss any mention of the cornfields, and only once does wheat appear. On the other hand the lovers' world is rich in fruits ; we hear much of vineyards, of figs, of apples and pomegranates. These imply a settled community, and the impression is borne out by the fact that the houses are solidly built, and not mere tents or booths. People know, too, what royalty is like, though it may be only from hearsay, for we get the impression that the gold, silver, ivory, costly woods and rich Tyrian dyes must have been a little remote from the ordinary life of the people who sang and heard these songs. In the exultation of his spirit the lover may feel himself to be a king, and the girl to be a queen. Indeed, there are good grounds for supposing that the title "Shulamite" does not refer to the village of Shunem, as is so often said, but is really no more than a feminine of Solomon. What can love not do ? Many waters cannot quench it and it is stronger than death ; it is not too much to expect that it should give the lovers the entry into an empire of the soul. It sheds a radiance over the one-storey cottage and the muddy village street, over the burning noon-day sun and the watchful toil of the shepherd's life.

To what date, or rather to what period are we to assign these lyrics ? It may be said at once that there seems to be no valid ground for connecting them with Solomon. On the contrary, there are features which suggest a comparatively late date. The vocabulary is unique ; a large proportion of the words used are found nowhere else in the Bible. This may be due in part to the objects mentioned in some of the poems, e.g. the henna and nard which are symbols of fragrance. These might be explained as words common in ordinary speech which by accident have not been preserved elsewhere. But we notice that among them we find quite a number of foreign origin. Most of these appear to have come into the Hebrew vocabulary from Persian, and it is difficult to place their introduction before the time of Cyrus. The word describing Solomon's palanquin in 3 : 9 may be Persian but is equally likely to have been Greek in origin, and even in that language it is not known before the latter part of the fourth century B.C. One curious feature is the relative pronoun. That which is normal in Biblical Hebrew appears only in the title to the book, 1 : 1 ; elsewhere the form used is that which is almost invariable in post-Biblical Hebrew and common only in Ecclesiastes in the Bible itself, though it appears in a number of late Psalms. It is not, however, necessarily late, for it

occurs in one of the oldest monuments of Hebrew literature, the song of Deborah in Jud. 5. It may be dialectal,
and be characteristic of northern Israel, for it is similar
to the common form in Phoenician. Even this, however,
is not a decisive clue, for it is found three or four times in
Lamentations. Allowing for all considerations, we cannot place the compilation, and probably for the most part
the composition, of these poems earlier than the third
century B.C.

Whenever they arose, for sheer literary beauty there are
few parallels to these snatches of Hebrew lyric to be found
elsewhere in the world's poetic store. Quaint conceits
are not lacking ; who can fail to be delighted with such a
passage as 8 : 1 ff ? The girl wishes that her lover were
as her brother, that she might freely ignore conventional
restraints—kiss him in public, and take him when she
would to her own home. The picture of Solomon's
marvellous vineyard in 8 : 11 f, the vineyard which is
worth less to the true lover than his little rustic farm,
offers us a *motif* which recalls the old French lyric :

> " Si le roi m'avoit donné
> Paris sa grand'ville . . ."

and the Hebrew will not suffer by comparison.

Simplicity and a fresh beauty are outstanding characteristics of these poems. We, too, cannot but delight in
the cool dew of early morning, in the flowers which make
the pastures so rich in colour, in the fragrance of fruit
and blossoming tree, in the delicate shades of gold and
pink that spread over the ripening fig. Against this background, Theocritus, Vergil and even the Italian sonneteers
seem artificial and stilted, and it is, perhaps, only in the
cavalier poets, in Burns and at times in Heine, that the
modern reader will find anything approaching the charm
of these ancient Hebrew lyrics. But there is more

than freshness, there is also passion, deep and intense, such as that which inspired the best of the Shakespearean sonnets. The lover and his lass shew us their inmost soul, without shame and without reserve. It may be that it is only in Sappho that we shall find a combination of qualities which we may compare with what is so justly entitled the " Song of Songs."

Commentators and expositors may have been justified in seeking a spiritual interpretation for this book. But to many readers this will be forced, unnatural, and even impossible. The book remains to them an anthology of secular love poems. What, then, is its place in Holy Scripture ? Can we justify to ourselves its inclusion in a body of literature which is essentially religious, and deals primarily with our relation to God ? We may well be grateful to the ingenious Rabbinic scholarship which secured its preservation, even if we are unable to accept its views, for the world could ill have spared the book. But we may go further still, and find a valid reason why we should gladly accept these poems in a corpus of writings whose function is above all things to help men into fuller communion with God. That love which culminates in marriage is the deepest and holiest element in human physical nature. Sex is capable of extreme abuse, but that is just because it is capable also of the greatest heights of earthly experience. What this book has to tell us, more than anything else, is that this element in mankind is not outside the range of God's interest in us, that it may be and should be employed in accordance with His will in the concentration for a lifetime on a single human object. " Threescore queens and fourscore concubines and virgins without number " ? No ; " My dove, my undefiled, is but one."

LAMENTATIONS

We have already seen something of what a "dirge" meant in the ancient world. Originally, no doubt, a funeral spell intended to keep the dead in his place and prevent him from annoying the living, it gradually developed into a genuine expression of the grief felt by survivors at the loss of one whom they loved. We may suppose that there were traditional and conventional formulae which would serve both purposes, and we gather from such a passage as Jer. 9 : 17 ff. that there was a recognized profession, composed of women, who went through a regular course of training in their work. They had to know the right words which would both allay the spirit of the dead and excite the tears of the living. Authorship of these dirges, however, was not necessarily confined to the professional women, and in II Chron. 35 : 25 we have a statement to the effect that Jeremiah composed a dirge over Josiah, together with a reference to a book of dirges.

It is, perhaps, this note which has given rise to the tradition that Jeremiah was the actual author of our present Book of Lamentations or "Dirges." It is beyond dispute that they, or some of them, are worthy of his poetic genius, and the book which bears his name attests the fact that he could and did compose works of this kind, cf. Jer. 9 : 19, 21. These, however, are very brief, comparable to the dirge of Amos over the fallen virgin of Israel (Am. 5 : 2), and are very different from the long and rather elaborate poems preserved in Lamentations. Occasionally, too, we have suggestions of a point of view which we can hardly associate with Jeremiah. When, for example, the poet in Lam. 5 : 7 lays the blame for Judah's disasters on an earlier generation, he is directly contradicting the principle which Jeremiah laid down in Jer. 31 : 29-30, where the prophet insists that the sinner alone must suffer for his wrongdoing— a doctrine to be more fully developed by Ezekiel. Again, Lam. 4 : 20 clearly refers to the ruined and captured king, and we can hardly imagine Jeremiah speaking of Zedekiah thus :

" The breath of our nostrils, the anointed of the Lord,
    Was taken in their pits,
Of whom we said, under his shadow
    We shall live among the nations."

But while we may find it impossible to accept the tradidition which ascribes the book to Jeremiah, there is abundant reason for assigning it, or part of it, to the age in which he lived, and to use it as a historical document illustrating the calamity which he had foreseen for forty years before it fell.

For the book is not a unity ; it does not pretend to be. It is a collection of five poems, four of them dirges in the strict sense, and the fifth a Psalm such as Israel's poets often uttered in times of distress. Each has its own literary characteristics, and internal evidence makes it practically certain that they are not all the work of a single author. They are not of equal literary merit, and they vary a good deal in the intensity of their feeling. While the first four, at any rate, may reasonably be referred to the siege of Jerusalem by Nebuchadrezzar, to the fall of the city and to its consequent desolation, we get the impression that some are nearer than others to actual disasters which they describe.

Chs. 1–4 are acrostic poems, though no two of them are exactly alike in their construction. In chs. 1, 2 and 4, the poet has assigned a stanza to each letter, but it occurs only at the head of the first line in the stanza. In ch. 3, as in Ps. 119, the poem falls into groups of three lines each, one group to every letter, and each line of the group begins with the proper letter. At the same time, the groups are not stanzas in the same sense as they are in 1, 2 and 4, since it is possible for the sense to be continued from one group to another, and the first line of a letter-group may be more closely associated with what precedes than with what follows. The verse-division in the English versions reflects this difference, for in chs. 1, 2 and 4 each letter-group is counted as a single verse, while in ch. 3 every line stands by itself. Thus chs. 1, 2 and 3 have the same number of lines, though the first two have only 22 verses while the third has 66.

Looking at these external characteristics we note that the four poems take the following forms :

Ch. 1 is an acrostic poem in which a stanza of three lines begins with its appropriate letter. The order of the alphabet is that which is now universally adopted, and goes back to ancient times.

Ch. 2 is also an acrostic poem in which a stanza of three lines begins with its appropriate letter, but the order of the alphabet differs slightly from the normal, since the letter פ (Pe), usually the seventeenth, comes before ע (Ayin), usually the sixteenth (the common arrangement may be seen in those Bibles which print the Hebrew letters at the head of each stanza in Ps. 119).

Ch. 3 is an acrostic in which three lines all begin with

the same letter. Here, as in ch. 2, the usual order of
ע, פ is reversed.

Ch. 4 is an acrostic in which a stanza of two lines is
assigned to each letter. Otherwise it resembles ch. 2.

The metre in all these is that which seems most
appropriate to the dirge, i.e., 3 : 2 varied occasionally
with 2 : 2. It was, in fact, in this book that a definite
metre, of the kind now generally admitted first attained
wide acceptance, and though earlier students recognized
only the 3 : 2 (a theory which led to some curious results),
it received the name of Qinah, or " dirge," metre. It
was not till long afterwards that it was noticed in other
poems which could not possibly be classed as " dirges,"
e.g., in Ps. 23.

The first poem gives us a picture of the desolation of
Jerusalem and of her people. It opens with the characteristic Hebrew groan—How ! It is not a question, it is an
exclamation of suffering, and stands outside the metrical
scheme of the verse. This " anacrusis " is not infrequently used by the Hebrew poets to give emotional
emphasis to what follows. The first line gives the key to
the whole poem ; the city that was once so great and
beautiful, the place that once stood so high in the esteem
of the peoples, has now fallen to the depths. Once
populous, now she is lonely, for her inhabitants are gone.
She had been powerful, now she is no more than a widow.
She had been the mistress of others, and now she herself
has to submit to forced labour, like any subject tribe.
As we read we see more and more of the desolation. The
land about her is deserted, for its people have been carried
away captive, and her own inhabitants too have gone
with them. She can find neither comfort nor sympathy
from those about her ; they mock at her and glory in her
fall. The poet owns that her troubles are a just punish-

ment for her sins, and in them he sees the hand of Yahweh at work. He cannot imagine that Yahweh is helpless, but He has not even protected His own sanctuary. Priests and elders, the chiefs in Church and State, are alike helpless, and perish of starvation. Yahweh, whom she has offended, is her only hope, and to Him she appeals for aid and restoration.

As we read this deeply moving expression of sorrow, we are struck by the fact that there is little or no reference to the actual horrors of siege and sack. It is the result of the fall of the city, not the terrible event itself, which fills the poet's mind. We shall realize this more fully when we come to glance at some of the other poems, and it has an important bearing on the date of the poem. It goes without saying that it must be placed earlier than any attempt to restore Jerusalem, and comes, therefore, from the time of the exile. But it is not to be placed near the beginning of that period. The first keen anguish has died away, and left a dull aching sorrow. Though there may never have been elsewhere pain like the pain of Jerusalem, it is no new thing; the wound is far from freshly inflicted. We might almost say that she was growing accustomed to her desolation, and it is a condition rather than a disastrous event which gives rise to the poet's utterance. In spite of the somewhat artificial flavour which an acrostic inevitably produces, the language has a solemn beauty, and whether we will or no we are carried back into the actual circumstances which called the dirge forth. The poem stands high among the world's lyrics of sorrow.

Ch. 2 may well be thought to stand even higher. In form, as we have seen, it closely resembles ch. 1, differing only in the places taken by two letters of the alphabet. Like the first poem, the second is a cry of woe and desolation, but it is much nearer to the actual disaster. The poet still remembers keenly incidents of the siege, the famine which destroyed more people than the weapons of the enemy, the corpses lying about the streets, the slaughter even of sacred persons, the cannibalism of mothers driven mad by hunger. It is not so much the desolation which followed on the sack of Jerusalem as the fearful details of the siege and capture which have impressed themselves upon him. In other ways the general atmosphere is much the same as in ch. 1 ; we observe here also the heart-rending contrast between the glorious past and the ghastly present, the exultant mockery of jealous and hostile neighbours. An interesting feature of the poet's thought is the way in which he sees the hand of Yahweh in all that has happened. Take v. 17 for example :

> " Yahweh hath done that which he had devised ;
>   He hath fulfilled his word ;
> As he had commanded in days of old,
>   He hath cast down, pitiless ;
> And he hath caused the enemy to rejoice over thee,
>   He hath set up the horn of thine adversaries."

Or again in v. 21, where Yahweh is directly addressed :

> " They lie on the ground in the streets—
>   Young and old ;
> My virgins and my young men
>   Are fallen by the sword ;
> Thou hast slain in the day of thine anger,
>   Thou hast slaughtered, hast not pitied."

Even Yahweh's sanctuary has not been spared :

> " And he hath done violence to his tabernacle as it were a
>   garden,
>   He hath destroyed his place of assembly ;

Yahweh hath caused to be forgotten in Zion
    Solemn assembly and sabbath,
And hath despised in the indignation of his anger
    King and priest." (v. 6).

Truly " Yahweh has become as an enemy " (v. 5). It
is rather striking that, in these circumstances, there is
little or no reference to the sins, either of the fathers or
of the generation which actually suffered the horrors
which the poet had seen. There can be no doubt that
he had seen them ; his feeling is too keen to let us think
that he was relying on tradition or on hearsay. What
is more, they were comparatively fresh in his memory.
There is a great difference between the emotional tone of
this chapter and that of ch. 1. Both are steeped in pain,
but here the poignant agony of grief has not yet settled
down into the ache of sorrow. We must place this poem
very near the beginning of the exilic period.

When we reach ch. 3 we are conscious at once of being
in an entirely different atmosphere. The metre is still
that of the Qinah, but this by no means compels us to
regard the poem as a dirge. The use of the acrostic
letter at the beginning of each of the three lines assigned to
it gives an artificial air to the whole. The gloom is
far from being so intense as it was in the first two chapters.
Vv. 25-27, for example, all begin with the word " good."
This may be due in part to the demands of the acrostic, for
comparatively few Hebrew words start with the letter
ט (t̤), and acrostic writers often have to fall back on
" ṭobh," the common Hebrew word for " good."
But we have other signs of a more hopeful attitude than
appears in other chapters. It seems clear that the poet
either has found, or expects to find in the near future,
release from his troubles and vengeance on his enemies.
There is, too, a certain lack of detail, a vagueness in

speaking of the distress into which the poet has fallen, which contrasts very strongly with the wealth of detail offered us by other poems in the book. Occasionally we get hints of quotation from other writings ; the opening words of v. 28 suggest an acquaintance with 1 : 1. It is surely not too fanciful to see in v. 30 a reminiscence of Is. 50 : 6. We naturally recall Jer. 9 : 1 on reading v. 48, and with vv. 12-13 we may compare Job 6 : 4, 16 : 12. The fact is that this poem is not a " dirge " at all, even in the somewhat wide sense which allows the term to include laments over cities and communities as well as over individuals. It belongs to the same class as a number of the Psalms, especially to those which cry out for deliverance from the threats of an enemy. There is confession of sin in v. 42, though the precise type of offence is not specified. The whole would be very suitable for use on some fast day, proclaimed as a result of national disaster in order to recover the favour of Yahweh and so win deliverance and triumph.

The date of this poem is not easy to determine. The passages which remind us of other writings are never direct quotations, though their language gives us good ground for supposing that this poet was acquainted with them. It is difficult to associate the piece with the fall of Jerusalem at all, and, as we have seen, we have to admit the possibility that it is even later than the book of Job. That would probably carry it down to a point rather late in the fourth century B.C. At the same time the parallels may be accidental, however unlikely this may seem at first sight, and in that case the poem may be earlier.

With ch. 4 we are back once more in the atmosphere of 586 B.C. The poem differs from ch. 2 mainly in having a two-line instead of a three-line stanza, but in other respects the two are closely similar and may be the work of the same poet. There is, perhaps, a tendency to dwell rather more on the horrors of the siege, and especially on the reaction of the women and children. The pitiful condition of these little ones appealed to the poet strongly. He has seen them suffering the agonies of thirst, perishing of hunger, and calling for the food which none can give. Little babies cry out at their mothers' dry breasts, and older children appeal in vain to their fathers for bread. Still more horrible is the cannibalism to which the starving women were reduced, slaughtering, cooking and eating even their own offspring. Incidentally it may be noted that Josephus records similar occurrences during the final siege of Jerusalem in A.D. 70. The poet feels strongly, too, the contrast between what was and what is. In former times the city had been rich in many ways, some had lived in real luxury, and, still more, her people had been beautiful and strong. Now all was changed :

" They that did feed delicately
　　Are desolate in the streets :
They that were brought up in scarlet
　　Embrace dunghills." (v. 5.)
" Their visage is blacker than coal ;
　　They are not known " (i.e. not recognisable)
　　　　　　" in the streets :
Their skin cleaveth to their bone ;
　　It is withered, it is become as a stick." (v. 8.)

In vv. 18-20 we live again through the actual fall of the city. The enemy is already through the walls, and, sword in hand, hunts down the wretched inhabitants, chasing them through the streets. The king, as we hear elsewhere, made his way out of the city and fled towards Jordan. The language of the poet suggests that he was among the small group who got away with Zedekiah, for he speaks as if the pursuit had been swift behind himself. He seems, too, to have been a faithful attendant on his royal master, for the climax of the disaster is reached when the enemy overtakes and captures the " breath of our nostrils, the anointed of Yahweh."

While the leading *motif* is the actual suffering, there is room for some reflection, and the poet realises that the punishment now fallen on Jerusalem is due to sin. But it is especially the sin of those who should have led the people to righteousness, the prophets and the priests (v. 13), which is responsible, for they " have shed the blood of the just in the midst of her." A study of the utterances delivered by Jeremiah will bear out this point of view, and will help to reinforce the strong impression, which we get from all sides of the matter, that this poem is the work of one who had lived through the great catastrophe and was writing while its details were still fresh in his mind.

Ch. 5 stands apart from the other four in several ways. Its metre is 3 : 3, not that of the Qinah, and it is not an acrostic poem. It does, however, contain 22 verses, the right number for an acrostic. Perhaps a writer of such pieces wrote his poem first as it came into his mind, and then went over it again, substituting for the first word in each verse one which began with the appropriate letter. The chapter may, then, have been written for acrostic treatment and been left incomplete, i.e., without the final process.

In general character it is nearer to ch. 3 than to any of the others. It is a picture of desolation and distress, of a people worn by famine and groaning under the yoke. Once only is there reference to the plight of the city itself, and that is couched in quite general terms—Zion is desolate and wild animals wander over the ruined site.

But we hear nothing of the process by which this came about, no word of siege or slaughter at the hands of an enemy. The nearest thing is the treatment of the women described in v. 11. There is nothing which speaks directly of exile, though some of the language might well have been used by Jewish captives in Mesopotamia. The old social and political order has broken up, and those who once had been the most prominent among the people have either disappeared or been reduced to degrading labour. There is constant danger from violence, but it does not seem to be the more or less organized persecution of a tyrannous conqueror, but rather that which arises from the presence of marauding and thievish bands.

In a word, the conditions are those which we know to have prevailed in the later period of the exile, and, to some extent, after the first return to Palestine. There may have been other ages in the post-exilic history to which the poem might be referred, but, in so far as we have details, there is none that fits it better than the latter part of the sixth century.

We may sum up. Lamentations consists of five poems, of varying authorship and of different dates. The only thing they have in common is that they are poems written in deep distress, though this is far more intense in some cases than in others. All may, and some must, be assigned to the period of the exile, and all appear to have been written in Palestine. Two of them, chs. 2 and 4, are very early in the period, and come from a time immediately after the fatal siege of Jerusalem. They may even be the work of the same writer, for both shew a superlative degree of poetic excellence. A little behind these two, both in time and in quality, comes ch. 1, whose date may be roughly between 570 and 560 B.C.

Finally, not earlier than the end of the exilic period, we have ch. 5, and, possibly, ch. 3, though this, if any, is likely to be later than the return from the exile. It is noticeable, too, that these two poems fall some way below the high artistic standard reached by the rest—again we feel that ch. 3 stands even after ch. 5. This does not mean that these two pieces are on a low level as compared with work of similar tone, either in Hebrew or in other literature. They are well up to the average, and the book, small as it is, remains the classic example of literary beauty rising out of the deepest suffering.

BIBLIOGRAPHY

THE following bibliography, which is restricted for the most part to works published during the last fifty years, makes no claim to completeness. It is designed simply as a guide to further reading on the part of the beginner, and thus represents but a small selection from the many works which need to be consulted by the more advanced student. Similarly, while reference is made to a number of French and German works, the student whose reading is restricted to English has been kept primarily in mind. An obelisk (†) denotes a Roman Catholic publication.

For the sake of background one should know something of the literature of the Old Testament as a whole, and several suitable introductions are available. Driver, *An Introduction to the Literature of the Old Testament*, 9th edit. rev. (1913), remains indispensable for the English reader ; but as it is considerably out of date, it should be supplemented by Oesterley & Robinson, *An Introduction to the Books of the Old Testament* (1934). The following are also recommended : Gautier, *Introduction à l'Ancien Testament*, 2nd edit. rev. (1914), 3rd edit. (1939) ; Eissfeldt, *Einleitung in das Alte Testament* (1934) ; Sellin, *Einleitung in das Alte Testament*, 7th edit. rev. (1935), also available in an English translation of the 3rd edition by Montgomery, i.e. *Introduction to the Old Testament* (1923) ; Weiser, *Einleitung in das Alte Testament* (1939) ; and Pfeiffer, *Introduction to the Old Testament* (1941). Attractive treatments of the literature in its historical development will be found in Bewer, *The Literature of the Old Testament*, 2nd edit. rev. (1933), and Hempel, *Die althebräische Literatur und ihr hellenistisch-jüdisches Nachleben* (1930-4). An outstanding feature of the works by Eissfeldt, Hempel, and Weiser is the attention paid to 'form-criticism.' Cf., for example, Chapters III and VII of this book. Finally, for an appreciation of the Old Testament as literature, see Sands, *Literary Genius of the Old Testament* (1926) ; and Macdonald, *The Hebrew Literary Genius* (1933).

The reader should also know something of the culture of ancient Israel and, indeed, of the ancient Near East in general ; and for this purpose one cannot do better than consult Lods, *Israël des origines au milieu du viiie siècle* (1930), and *Les prophètes d'Israël et les débuts du Judaïsme* (1935), both of which are obtainable in an English translation by Hooke, i.e., *Israel from its Beginnings to the Middle of the Eighth Century* (1932), and *The Prophets and the Rise of Judaism* (1937). Two important Danish studies are also available in an English translation, i.e., Pedersen, *Israel : its Life and Culture, I-II* (1926) and *III-IV* (1940) ; and these too may be strongly recommended, provided that they are read with caution.

The foregoing may be supplemented by Gressmann, *Altorientalische Texte und Bilder zum Alten Testament*, 2nd edit. rev. (1926-7) : and (a) the relevant sections in *The Cambridge Ancient History*, edit. Bury, Cook, etc. (1923-39) ; Oesterley & Robinson, *A History of Israel* (1932) ; Schofield, *The Historical Background of the Bible* (1938) ; H. Wheeler Robinson, *The History of Israel : its Facts and Factors*, in this series (1938) ; Wright & Filson, *The Westminster Historical Atlas to the Bible* (1945) ; (b) H. Wheeler Robinson, *The Religious Ideas of the Old Testament*, in this series (1913) ; Oesterley & Robinson, *Hebrew Religion : its Origin and Development*, 2nd edit. rev. (1937) ; Schofield, *The Religious Background of the*

Bible (1944) ; Snaith, *The Distinctive Ideas of the Old Testament* (1944) ; (c) Bertholet, *Kulturgeschichte Israels* (1919), available in an English translation by Dallas, i.e., *A History of Hebrew Civilization* (1926) ; J. M. P. Smith, *The Moral Life of the Hebrews* (1923) ; Kennett, *Ancient Hebrew Social Life and Custom as indicated in Law, Narrative and Metaphor*, Schweich Lectures for 1931 (1933).

The following general studies are also recommended : Dodd, *The Authority of the Bible* (1928) ; *Myth and Ritual*, edit. Hooke (1933) ; *The Labyrinth*, edit. Hooke (1935) ; Graham & May, *Culture and Conscience* (1936) ; Cook, *The Old Testament : a Reinterpretation* (1936), *The " Truth " of the Bible* (1938), and *An Introduction to the Bible* (1945) ; Hempel, *Gott und Mensch im Alten Testament*, 2nd edit. rev. (1936), and *Das Ethos des Alten Testaments* (1938) ; Causse, *Du groupe ethnique à la communauté religieuse* (1937) ; Albright, *From the Stone Age to Christianity* (1940) ; North, *The Old Testament Interpretation of History* (1946) ; H. Wheeler Robinson, *Inspiration and Revelation in the Old Testament* (1946) ; and Rowley, *The Re-discovery of the Old Testament* (1946).

N.B.—There is no satisfactory work in English on the theology of the Old Testament, although the posthumous work by Davidson, *The Theology of the Old Testament* (1904), should not be left out of account. Apart from this the reader must be referred to Eichrodt, *Theologie des Alten Testaments*, i (1933), ii (1935), iii (1939) ; or the much smaller works under the same title by Sellin, 2nd edit. (1936), and Köhler (1936).

In addition the reader will find many useful articles of a summary kind in (a) *The People and the Book*, edit. Peake (1925) ; *Record and Revelation*, edit. H. Wheeler Robinson (1938) ; *A Companion to the Bible*, edit. Manson (1939) and the Old Testament volumes in *The Clarendon*

Bible (1926-   ) : (b) *A New Commentary on Holy Scripture including the Apocrypha*, edit. Gore etc. (1929) ; *The Abingdon Bible Commentary*, edit. Eiselen etc. (1929) ; and *A Commentary on the Bible*, edit. Peake & Grieve, new edit. with supplement (1936).

Valuable material will also be found in the principal dictionaries and encyclopaedias, notably *Encyclopaedia Biblica*, edit. Cheyne & Black (1899-1903) ; *A Dictionary of the Bible*, edit. Hastings (1898-1904) ; *A Dictionary of the Bible*, edit. Hastings (1909), which is quite distinct from the foregoing larger work in five volumes ; and *The Encyclopaedia of Religion and Ethics*, edit. Hastings (1908-1926). Further, the advanced student cannot afford to neglect *Die Religion in Geschichte und Gegenwart*, edit. Gunkel & Zscharnack, 2nd edit. rev. (1927-32), and the many important articles on Old Testament subjects in *Theologisches Wörterbuch zum Neuen Testament*, edit. G. Kittel (1933-   ).

Finally, there are several *series* of commentaries which need to be consulted in connection with Chapters III-XI, although the reader must be warned that the quality of the individual volumes sometimes varies quite considerably. The following will be found represented in this selected bibliography : (a) *The Cambridge Bible for Schools and Colleges*, edit. Kirkpatrick (*CB*) ; *The Century Bible*, edit. Adeney (*Cent. B*) ; *The International Critical Commentary*, edit. Driver, etc. (*ICC*) ; *Westminster Commentaries*, edit. Lock & Simpson (*West. C*) ; (b) *Handbuch zum Alten Testament*, edit. Eissfeldt (*HAT*) ; *Handkommentar zum Alten Testament*, edit. Nowack (*HK*) ; *Kommentar zum Alten Testament*, edit. Sellin (*KAT*) ; and *Kurzer Hand-Commentar zum Alten Testament*, edit. Marti (*KHC*). Attention may also be drawn to *Die Heilige Schrift des Alten Testaments*, edit. Kautzsch & Bertholet,

4th edit. (1922-3) ; *Die Schriften des Alten Testaments,*
by Gunkel, Gressmann, etc., 2nd edit. (1921-5) ;
Exegetisches Handbuch zum Alten Testament,† edit. Nikel
& Schulz ; *Die Heilige Schrift des Alten Testaments,*†
edit. Feldmann & Herkenne.

CHAPTER I.—The following studies* in the fields of
English and German literature will be found useful for
comparative purposes : Saintsbury, *A History of English
Prosody from the Twelfth Century to the Present Day,* 3 vols.
(1906-10), and *Historical Manual of English Prosody* (1910) ;
Abercrombie, *Principles of English Prosody* (1923) ;
Richards, *Principles of Literary Criticism* (1925) ; and
Heusler, *Deutsche Versgeschichte, I : Einführendes ; Grund-
begriffe der Verslehre der Altgermanische Vers* (1925).

CHAPTER II.—Here the beginner will find it sufficient
to consult Budde, ' The Forms of Hebrew Poetry,' in
Hastings, *A Dictionary of the Bible* iv, pp. 3-9 ; Gray,
The Forms of Hebrew Poetry (1915) ; and Burney, *The
Poetry of our Lord* (1925), Chapter I, on ' The Formal
Characteristics of Hebrew Poetry.'

For a critical survey of the many attempts since
Lowth to define the principles underlying ancient Hebrew
poetry (e.g., the theories associated with the names of
Bellermann, Saalschütz, Ewald, Meier, Ley, Budde,
Bickell, Müller, Grimme, and Sievers), the advanced
student may be referred to Cobb, *A Criticism of Systems of
Hebrew Metre* (1905).

At the same time it should be borne in mind that the
whole question is still *sub judice*, and much important
material is to be found in the learned journals which are

---

* Kindly suggested by Professor E. C. Llewellyn of the Department of
English, University College, Cardiff.

devoted to biblical and allied subjects. Cf., for example, the survey by Begrich, ' Zur Hebräischen Metrik,' in *Theologische Rundschau*, N.F.4 (1932), pp. 67-89, which deals with developments in this field from the year 1907 to date.

Finally, for the poetic structure of the Ugaritic texts (with particular reference to parallelism), see Gordon, *Ugaritic Grammar*† (1940), pp. 78-87.

CHAPTER III.—For a detailed study of the passages discussed in the text the reader must be referred to the various commentaries which are listed, for example, in the above-mentioned introductions to the Old Testament by Eissfeldt, Oesterley & Robinson, and Pfeiffer.

On the general subject of this chapter there is little of value in English, but reference may be made to G. A. Smith, *The Early Poetry of Israel in Its Physical and Social Origins*, Schweich Lectures for 1910 (1912) ; and Oesterley, *Ancient Hebrew Poems* (1938). For the rest, see Causse *Les plus vieux chants de la Bible* (1926) ; Eissfeldt, *Einleitung*, pp. 69-137, and *Der Maschal im Alten Testament* (1913) ; and Jahnow, *Das hebräische Leichenlied im Rahmen der Völkerdichtung* (1923).

CHAPTERS IV-V. Of commentaries in English the beginner may use Peake, *Cent.B* (1905); Strahan, *The Book of Job Interpreted* (1913) ; Davidson, *CB*, new edit. rev. by Lanchester (1926) ; and Kissane, *The Book of Job*† (1939). In this connection the English translation in rhythmical form by McFadyen, *The Wisdom Books in Modern Speech* (1918), may also be recommended. For the more advanced student, however, Driver & Gray, *ICC* (1921), with its very full treatment of the relevant textual, philological, and exegetical problems, is indispensable. Ball, *The Book of Job* (1922), is a fresh and stimulating piece of work, but owing to its predominant philological interest and its bold treatment of the text it is primarily a work for the specialist. Of foreign commentaries the best are those of Duhm, *KHC* (1897), and Dhorme, *Le Livre de Job*† (1926), which is an exhaustive piece of work, and, like that of Driver & Gray, is of outstanding importance; but reference must also be made to Budde, *HK*, 2nd edit. (1913); König, *Das Buch Hiob* (1929); and Hölscher, *HAT* (1937).

For the English reader the following general studies will be found of value: Peake, *The Problem of Suffering in the Old Testament* (1904); H. Wheeler Robinson, *The Cross of Job* (1916); McFadyen, *The Problem of Pain: a Study in the Book of Job* (1917); Jastrow, *The Book of Job: its Origin, Growth and Interpretation* (1920); McKechnie, *Job: Moral Hero, Religious Egoist and Mystic* (1926); and Kraeling, *The Book of the Ways of God* (1938): but where possible these should be supplemented by Kautzsch, *Das sogenannte Volksbuch von Hiob* (1900); Sellin, *Das Problem des Hiobbuches* (1919); Baumgärtel, *Der Hiobdialog* (1933); and Lindblom, *Le composition du livre de Job* (1945). See also the general studies of Israel's wisdom literature which are cited below in connection with Chapter IX.

CHAPTERS VI-VIII.—For the English reader Kirkpatrick, *CB* (1902), is of special value. Within its limits it is a model piece of work; and though sadly out of date, it has yet to be superseded. It may be supplemented, however, by Oesterley, *The Psalms: Translated with Text-critical and Exegetical Notes* (1939). The philological notes in Briggs, *ICC* (1906-7), are sometimes useful; and Buttenwieser, *The Psalms: Chronologically*

Treated with a New Translation (1938), is interesting as an unconvincing attempt to arrange the psalms in their historical sequence. See also McFadyen, *The Psalms in Modern Speech* (1916), i.e., a companion volume to that which is noted above in connection with Chapters IV–V, *ad init.*

The best foreign commentaries are those of R. Kittel, *KAT*, 5th & 6th edit. (1929), which may be singled out for its fusion of careful scholarship and devotional exegesis ; and Gunkel, *HK* (1926), which is remarkable for its combination of wide reading and scholarly insight, though somewhat marred by an over-confidence in textual emendation : but the commentaries by Baethgen, *HK*, 3rd edit. (1904) Schmidt, *HAT* (1934), and Calès, *Le Livre des Psaumes*† (1936), have each their peculiar value.

Special studies in the Psalter may be represented by (a) Peters, *The Psalms as Liturgies* (1922) ; *The Psalmists*, edit. Simpson (1926) ; Welch, *The Psalter in Life, Worship and History* (1926) ; Snaith, *Studies in the Psalter* (1934) ; Cumming, *The Assyrian and Hebrew Hymns of Praise* (1934) ; Widengren, *The Accadian and Hebrew Psalms of Lamentation as Religious Documents* (1937) ; Oesterley, *A Fresh Approach to the Psalms* (1937) ; James, *Thirty Psalmists* (1938) ; and Patton, *Canaanite Parallels in the Book of Psalms* (1944) : (b) Gunkel, *Ausgewählte Psalmen*, 4th edit. rev. (1917) ; Mowinckel, *Psalmenstudien I–VI* (1921-4) ; Stummer, *Sumerisch-akkadische Parallelen zum Aufbau alttestamentlicher Psalmen*† (1922) ; Quell, *Das kultische Problem der Psalmen* (1926) ; Schmidt, *Die Thronfahrt Jahves* (1927), and *Das Gebet des Angeklagten im Alten Testament* (1928) ; Gunkel & Begrich, *Einleitung in die Psalmen* (1933) ; and Weiser, *Die Psalmen ausgewählt, übersetzt und erklärt*, 2nd edit. (1939).

CHAPTER IX.—The English reader has at his disposal two useful commentaries in Toy, *ICC* (1899), and Oesterley, *West. C* (1929), the latter having the merit of attempting to place the book of Proverbs in its setting within the general context of the wisdom literature of the ancient Near East. The English translation in rhythmical form by McFadyen, in *The Wisdom Books in Modern Speech*, as cited above in connection with Chapters IV-V, may also be recommended.

Of foreign commentaries, attention must be drawn to Gemser, *HAT* (1937), for the same reason as that given in the case of Oesterley. For the rest, it will be sufficient to mention Wildeboer, *KHC* (1897), and Frankenberg, *HK* (1898).

On the whole the book of Proverbs is better served by the many general or special studies which have been published in this field in recent years, particularly (a) Elmslie, *Studies in Life from Jewish Proverbs* (1917); Oesterley, *The Wisdom of Egypt and the Old Testament* (1927); Ranston, *The Old Testament Wisdom Books and Their Teaching* (1930); and Rankin, *Israel's Wisdom Literature : its Bearing on Theology and the History of Religion* (1936) : (b) Eissfeldt, as cited above in connection with Chapter III; Gressmann, *Israels Spruchweisheit im Zusammenhang der Weltliteratur* (1925); Humbert, *Recherches sur les Sources Égyptiennes de la Littérature Sapientiale d'Israël* (1929); Fichtner, *Die altorientalische Weisheit in ihrer israelitisch-jüdischen Ausprägung* (1933); Baumgartner, *Israelitische und altorientalische Weisheit* (1933); and Duesberg, *Les Scribes Inspirés : Introduction aux Livres Sapientiaux de la Bible*† (1938-9).

CHAPTER X.—There is no satisfactory, full-scale commentary in English on the Song of Songs. What little is available is noted below. In general see : (a) for the dramatic theories, Ewald, *Das Hohelied Salomo's* (1826) ; Renan, *Le Cantique des Cantiques* (1860) ; Delitzsch, *Hoheslied und Koheleth* (1875), available in an English translation by Easton, i.e., *Commentary on the Song of Songs and Ecclesiastes* (1877); Rothstein, *Das Hohe Lied* (1893) ; Hazan, *Le Cantique des Cantiques enfin expliqué* (1936) : also, as a series of dramatic lyrics or as a dramatic poem, Harper, *CB* (1902) ; Cannon, *The Song of Songs edited as a dramatic poem* (1913) ; and Pouget & Guitton, *Le Cantique des Cantiques†* (1934) : (b) for the wedding-cycle theory : Budde, *KHC* (1898) ; Siegfried, *HK* (1898) ; Martin, *Cent. B* (1908) : (c) for the love-lyric theory, Haupt, *Biblische Liebeslieder : das sogenannte Hohelied Salomos* (1907) ; Staerk, in *Die Schriften des Alten Testaments*, 2nd edit. (1920) ; Jastrow, *The Song of Songs, being a collection of love lyrics of Ancient Palestine* (1921) : (d) for the theory of an Adonis-Tammuz liturgy, Meek, ' Canticles and the Tammuz Cult,' in *American Journal of Semitic Languages and Literatures*, xxxix (1922-3), and in *The Song of Songs : a Symposium*, edit. Schoff (1924) ; Wittekindt, *Das Hohe Lied und seine Beziehungen zum Istarkult* (1926).

Finally, the beginner may be referred to Ranston, as cited above in connection with Chapter IX ; and for further reading the more advanced student should consult the fully documented article by Rowley, in *The Journal of Theological Studies*, xxxviii (1937), pp. 337-363, which also gives detailed references for the Jewish and Christian allegorical interpretations in both their ancient and their modern forms.

CHAPTER XI.—For the book of Lamentations the English reader is practically confined to Peake, *Cent. B*

(1912), and Streane, *CB* (1913). Of foreign commentaries the best are those of Budde, *KHC* (1898), and Lohr, *KH*, 2nd edit. (1907), on which those of Peake and Streane are largely dependent. See also Jahnow, as cited above in connection with Chapter III.

AUBREY R. JOHNSON.

INDEX

228